LETTERS FROM PRISON

JEFFERSON DAVIS TO HIS WIFE, 1865-1866

Edited by
Felicity Allen

Texas Review Press
Huntsville, Texas

FIRST EDITION, 2014

Requests for permission to reproduce material from this work should be sent
to:

Permissions
Texas Review Press
English Department
Sam Houston State University
Huntsville, TX 77341-2146

Acknowledgements:

I am eternally grateful to Dr. Donald Livingston for his encouragement of this project
and for his immense patience. Thanks are due also for help afforded me by the keeper
of the texts, B. J. Gooch, Special Collections Librarian at Transylvania, and two of my
granddaughters, Elizabeth Earnest of Auburn, Alabama, and Marian Bradshaw Adams
of Louisville, Kentucky, who helped with the typing. Michelle Rodriguez did a crucial bit
of searching in my papers at Beauvoir. My main printed help came from the beautifully
edited *Papers of JD*, Vol. 12. I could not have succeeded at all without the secretarial
assistance of my daughter, Mary Christine, and her husband, David Bradshaw, of
Lexington, Kentucky, with whom my husband, Ward Allen, and I made our home.
The bulk of the work, heroically offered, is that of the chief typist, Miss Mary Neyer of
Catawissa, Pennsylvania, who terms herself my "Copperhead friend." My best friend,
Christine Benagh—a deep-dyed Southerner born in New Jersey—kept me on track with
her prayers. With thanks to all who helped in any way.

Jefferson Davis Letter 121 courtesy of University Libraries Division of Special
Collections, The University of Alabama.

Library of Congress Cataloging-in-Publication Data

Davis, Jefferson, 1808-1889, author.
  [Correspondence. Selections]
  Letters from prison : Jefferson Davis to his wife / [compiled by] Felicity
Allen.
     pages cm
  Compilation of letters written by Jefferson Davis to his wife Varina Davis
while he was imprisoned in Fortress Monroe, Virginia, from October 1865
through April 1866.
   ISBN 978-1-937875-74-9 (paperback : alk. paper)
  1. Davis, Jefferson, 1808-1889--Correspondence. 2. Presidents--
Confederate States of America--Correspondence. 3. Statesmen--United
States--Correspondence. 4. Davis, Jefferson, 1808-1889--Captivity, 1865-
1866. 5. Davis, Jefferson, 1808-1889--Family. I. Allen, Felicity, 1924-
compiler. II. Davis, Varina, 1826-1906, addressee. III. Title.
  E467.1.D26A4 2014
  973.713092--dc23
                                                          2014023202

I dedicate this work, in general, to all who love the South, so that they may see what manner of man their leader was; and in particular to Miss Mary Neyer of Catawissa, Pennsylvania, my chief (and pro bono) typist, who calls herself my "Copperhead friend."

Table of Contents

Images

Introduction

The Letters bundled here hang naturally together: All are written from one person to another, always the same persons. The place named in the dateline is invariable: Fortress Monroe, Virginia. The dates (August 21, 1865-April 23, 1866) bind these missives in a span of eight months. Then there is a little note later which ties them together even more surely. All of this gives us a unity of time and space and action reminiscent of classic European drama. There is plenty of drama; these are some of the most turbulent months in American history. We are spared tragedy by the character of the protagonist.

When our Letters begin, American society has been torn apart by what is now called, inaccurately, "The Civil War," or worse, "The Rebellion"; but is more aptly known as "The War for Southern Independence" or "The War of Northern Aggression"; or simply, "The War Between the States." (How about "The Late Unpleasantness"?)

To Southerners who had suffered most, it was simply *The War*. Now the equally bitter—some say more bitter—period known as "Reconstruction" is underway. The fighting ended in either April or May of 1865, depending on whether you take for the end the surrender of the two main Southern armies led by Generals Robert E. Lee and Joseph E. Johnston (April), or the capture of the President of the Confederate States of America (May).

President Jefferson Davis (from now on, JD) is the sole author of our Letters. In May of 1865, he was on a journey (he would never call it "flight") from his country's capital, Richmond, Virginia, to his Trans-Mississippi Department. "Mississippi" here means the River. Cross it, going west, and you find yourself in the vast Department comprising acreage from lesser States and a Territory and the absolute whole of Texas. He hoped to find there a body of troops still organized enough to continue the fight for a separate country of Southern States.

Davis was probably capable of leading such a force himself. He was trained in war-making at West Point, receiving his commission as Second Lieutenant of Infantry in 1828. When he heard of a cavalry unit forming, he asked for, and got, a transfer to it.

So it was as a First Lieutenant of Dragoons that he resigned from the U.S. Army in 1835 to marry and become a planter. He kept his interest in the Army. When his wife died, he became an omnivorous reader. By 1845 he knew all about the new rifles that were so much better than the old muskets. When he was elected colonel of the Mississippi regiment volunteering for the war with Mexico, he insisted that every infantryman be armed with this superior weapon, so he became Colonel of the First Mississippi Rifles. They made him a hero when they broke a charge of Mexican cavalry at Buena Vista. In 1861, his fame earned him the leadership of all Mississippi troops with the rank of major-general.

He was waiting to take command when he was called to a less agreeable duty: political head for the forming nation. He'd had plenty of practice for that too, having served the United States in both the House and the Senate, and in the cabinet of President Franklin Pierce as Secretary of War (1853-1857).

In 1845 David had remarried. The First Lady of the Confederacy was Varina Banks Howell Davis (from now on VHD). She is the sole recipient of these prison Letters and the little extra note. She had left Richmond several days before it fell to the Yankees. Her husband had insisted that she take their children to a safer place. He had sent his private secretary, Burton N. Harrison, as her escort. There were four Davis children then: Margaret (called Maggie or Polly), ten years old; Jeff Jr., eight and a half; William (Billy), three and a half; and Varina Anne, a babe in arms, (nicknamed Pie; Piecake; Li'l Pie; L.P.; and, finally, Winnie or Winnanne). There had been two more children. The first, Samuel Emory, had died of an unknown disease before he was two years old; and Joseph Evan had fallen recently from a high balustrade behind the Confederate White House in Richmond, dying from his injuries at the age of five, in 1864. These children, both living and dead, occupy the thoughts of their parents all through our Letters.

There was a fifth child on the road with Varina, a black orphan about five years old—called in the accounts of him both "negro" and "mulatto"— whom Varina had rescued from cruelty on a Richmond street and taken into the White House to live. VHD in her wonderfully detailed history, *Jefferson Davis... a Memoir by his Wife*, tells how the boy called himself "Jim Limber" in his everyday clothes, but in his best suit on Sunday said he was "Jeems Henry Brooks." The suit was for church-going. The Davises belonged to St. Paul's Episcopal Church across from Capitol Square. The frequent *"BCP"* in the notes to our Letters refers to the Episcopal *Book of Common Prayer.*

We will find JD in prison reading every day the regular church services (Morning Prayer and Evening Prayer); on some days the Litany and the Communion Service; and every night the wholly different set of Family Prayers designed for use at home. He uses the Tables in the front of the Book to find what Bible lessons and Psalms to read. A separate list gives him readings for feast days. The Bible passages are all in the King James Version, except for Psalms. The Psalter in the *BCP* is the earlier translation of Miles Coverdale (1549).

VHD was not sure, with the world in flux around her now, what to do with her helpless little charges. Her sister, Margaret Howell, at least was there to help. VHD had a vague hope of taking ship for Europe, where she could get proper schooling for the children—always a foremost concern with the Davises. Her train now consisted of several mule wagons and a little covered wagon called an "ambulance," in which the family rode, with a number of paroled Southern soldiers on their own horses both escorting VHD and going home. Their pace, always west/southwest, was necessarily slow.

Unknown to them, JD was following their route on horseback. He had dismissed the military units who had guarded his route from North Carolina, and now had only ten men with him as he moved through middle Georgia. He had stayed in Richmond till the last moment. Then on the very last train out, he had brought as many official papers and as many officials as he could. These men kept the Confederate government going for several weeks. We meet these men and many others of the "Lost Cause" in the Letters. Judah Benjamin, a true Davis friend, and the South's last Secretary of State, came with him but soon found his rotund figure unsuited to horseback, and set out for the Gulf Coast behind wheels, planning to reach the Trans-Mississippi by boat. George Davis

(Attorney General) and George Trenholm (Secretary of the Treasury) left the party for good reasons, but were captured elsewhere later. John H. Reagan (Postmaster General) and Frank Lubbock, JD's aide-de-camp specialist on the Trans-Mississippi (governor of Texas 1861-63) were already heading homeward, yet they made a pact between them never to leave JD, but to share whatever his fate was to be.

It was to be captured. He had overtaken his wife's little caravan only a few days before. His men fretted about the slow pace of the wagons, so he led them westward rapidly once more. Then rumors reached them of a plan to attack the wagon train. They hurried back to ensure the family's safety. While they were camped for the night, Yankee soldiers surrounded them.

The soldiers were jubilant when they found that they had captured the President. It meant they would get the gold promised in a proclamation by the new U.S. president, Andrew Johnson. The proclamation also announced to the world, without a shred of evidence, that JD was suspected of complicity in the murder of Abraham Lincoln, which had occurred on April 14. Davis knew he was innocent. He also knew that to say so to these people now would be, in a favorite phrase of his, "worse than useless."

These same soldiers took their prisoners, who now included C. S. Vice President Alexander H. Stephens and the ex-senator from Alabama, Clement Clay, and his wife, Virginia, to the coast at Savannah. Then an ocean-going steamer, the *Clyde*, took them up the East Coast to Hampton Roads, where their destination, Fortress Monroe, loomed.

Most of the prisoners were sent to other strongholds. Stephens was jailed in Boston Harbor. Burton Harrison found himself in Washington D.C. among those being tried for Lincoln's death; finally he was locked up at the Fort Delaware jail.

The prisoners were kept waiting on the *Clyde* for several days while two stone gun emplacements in the fort were turned into two little cells—one for Clay, one for Davis—complete with iron bars and guard rooms so arranged that the prisoners would always be in sight. No one could speak to them or shake their hand, and soldiers were to pace within the little cells day and night. We can see in our Letters something of the effect on them of this loss of all privacy and all normal contact with other people. They were entering the harrowing trial of solitary confinement. Just before Davis was taken from the *Clyde* to this living tomb, embracing Varina for the last time, he whispered his response to the Proclamation: "No matter what evidence the North may adduce, remember my dying testimony to you is that I had no part in assassination."

Clement Clay was the only other man named with Davis in the Proclamation as a conspirator, with the same price on his head. The moment he heard that the United States was trying to smear him with the death of Lincoln, Clay immediately went to the nearest U. S. army post and gave himself up. He had been about to set out for the Trans-Mississippi, but he knew he was innocent of this charge and felt compelled to say so. The post Clay found was at Macon, Georgia, the very one to which the Davis party was being escorted. Poor Clay! The soldiers seemed to be interested only in the gold offered for his capture. To make sure they got it, they said they had "arrested" him, and treated him like a dangerous criminal.

Clay and Davis were old friends from their U. S. Senate days, when they represented Alabama and Mississippi. Clay had often visited and read to Davis when he was desperately ill in 1858. Clay soon lay very sick in the prison. Surely Davis remembered and wished to do the same for Clay when he wrote Varina, "I earnestly desired to be with him."

Though the manuscripts of the letters are deposited at JD's alma mater, Transylvania University in Lexington, Kentucky, there is one additional communication in the Varina Davis papers at the University of Alabama. The item is dated September 21, 1866—five months after the last full Letter in our set. This tiny triangle folded from a single small sheet of writing paper creates its own envelope. It is addressed not to "Varina Davis," but to "Mrs. Jefferson Davis," and not to somewhere in Georgia, but to "Carroll Hall." But Carroll Hall was located within Fortress Monroe! It was the quarters for artillery officers coming to learn how to manage the big coastal guns. The place in the dateline, for once, is not *Fortress Monroe*, it is *Prison*.

This dateline tells us so much: there have been no letters since April because Varina has won her heart's desire, cherished through every letter, every repulse, every disappointment—she is with her husband and has a place to live within the fort. The body of the note reveals that Pie Cake is with her. So why does JD suddenly say "Prison"? Because, though Varina has worked wonders getting permission for JD to go within the fort where he pleases during the day, still at night he has to go back to his prison cell, the same small stone enclosure where he has endured all these months. Soon he will have a new wooden cell in Carroll Hall itself. The next step will find the Davises living in an apartment together there, even entertaining the friends who visit. This little piece of paper allows us to pass through all the sadness in the letters knowing that, just as JD says over and over, everything will turn out right because God is in charge. Eventually the Davises will be released, reunited with their older children, and will spend many years enjoying the quiet life they look forward to in the Letters.

Jeff and Varina Davis look out on a changing world. They look out on their society which has been blown to bits by The War. Before it, they lived on their own land in the house they built. Now they are homeless and poor. They have lost everything material, but they still have each other and the family. They have a lot to say about that broken world. The piece-by-piece revelation of their relations with their servants alone would repay our reading. Only Jeff's words are printed, and, yet, Varina's voice is mirrored in his, they are so close. Listen to them.

Jefferson Davis's prose is of an excellent order—strong and clear and at times beautiful. See his description of *The Iliad*. We allow him all his nineteenth-century peculiarities: we pass over "your's" for "yours"; we keep "myself" and "yourself" where we would use "me" and "you"; and we let innumerable comma faults slip by. It is evident even in these few Letters that his style is enriched by a lifetime of reading classic works of British and American history and literature and is kept fresh by acquaintance with popular novelists, from Mary Shelley through Dickens and Thackery.

As editor of this series of Letters, my ambition has been to present them exactly as they are in the original manuscripts at Transylvania, word for word as they came from the hand of Jefferson Davis. Some explanatory notes of mine are always set off by brackets, not to be confused with JD's fine prose. Only in the first Letter do I point out all the rough places and the afterthoughts written between the lines in JD's tiny, precise script. This is because they seem to reflect his illness at that time. Other interesting peculiarities are the double-written pages where the primary message is crossed at right angles by an overlying set of words conveying a totally different message;

and JD's abbreviations of his own signature, nailed by the two dots, never missing (well, hardly ever): See the "Illustrations" pages. I believe this is the first printing of all these interrelated twenty Letters, each in its entirety. I remember, as I aim at absolute accuracy, the remark of A. E. Housman about his poems in this regard: "Vain hope." Yet I hope on and check my transcriptions one more time.

I am eternally grateful to Dr. Donald Livingston for his encouragement of this project and for his immense patience. Thanks are due also for help afforded me by the keeper of the texts, B. J. Gooch, Special Collections Librarian at Transylvania, and two of my granddaughters, Elizabeth Earnest of Auburn, Alabama, and Marian Bradshaw Adams of Louisville, Kentucky, who helped with the typing. Michelle Rodriguez did a crucial bit of searching in my papers at Beauvoir. My main printed help came from the beautifully edited *Papers of J.D.*, Vol. 12, which deals with our Letters. I could not have succeeded at all without the secretarial assistance of my daughter, Mary Christine, and her husband, David Bradshaw, of Lexington, Kentucky, with whom my husband, Ward Allen, and I made our home while I worked on this book. The bulk of the work, heroically offered, is that of the chief typist, Miss Mary Neyer of Catawissa, Pennsylvania, who terms herself my "Copperhead friend." My best friend, Christine Benagh—a deep-dyed Southerner born in New Jersey—kept me on track with her prayers. With thanks to all who helped in any way.

Felicity Allen
Lexington, Kentucky
May A.D. 2013

Needlepoint made by Varina Davis for Jefferson Davis

LETTERS FROM PRISON

JEFFERSON DAVIS TO HIS WIFE, 1865-1866

Letter 1
(August 21, 1865)

Fortress Monroe Va
Aug. 21, 1865

My Dear Wife,

I am now permitted to write to you, under two conditions viz: that I confine myself to family matters, and that my letter shall be examined by the U.S. Atty. Genl.[1] before it is sent to you.

This will sufficiently explain to you the omission of subjects on which you would desire me to write. I presume it is however permissible for me to relieve your disappointment in regard to my silence on the subject of future action towards me, by stating that of the purpose of the authorities I know nothing.

To morrow it will be three months since we were suddenly and unexpectedly separated, and many causes prominent among which has been my anxiety for you and our children have made that quarter in seeming duration long, very long. I sought permission to write to you that I might make some suggestions as to your movements and as to domestic arrangements. The first and most important point has in the mean time been so far decided by the journey of the older children that until a key is furnished to open what is now to me unintelligible I can only speak in very general terms, in regard to your future movements. It is to be inferred that you have decided and I think wisely not to return to our old home[2], at least in the present disturbed condition of society. Thus you have the world before you but not where to choose, as the loss of our property will require the selection to be, with a view to subsistence. Should I regain my liberty before our "people" have become vagrant there are many of them whose labor I could direct so as to make it not wholly unprofitable. Their good faith under many trials, and the mutual affection between them and myself make [*me* (*Intl.*)] always solicitous for their welfare and probably keeps them expectant of my coming. Should my fate be not to return to that country you can best be advised by Brother Jos[3]: as to what and how [*it should be attempted, if any thing may be done* (*Intl.*)] Always understand however that I do not mean that you should attempt in person to do any thing in the matter. I often think of "old Uncle Bob" and always with painful anxiety. If Sam. has rejoined him he will do all in his power for the old man's comfort and safety.

The Smith land had better be returned to the heirs. No deed was made and the payments were for moveable [*effects* (*Intl. above cancelled* "*property*")] and for interest; their right to the [*land which alone remains* (*Intl. above another cancelled* "*property*" *and* "*is*")] therefore clearly [*revives* (*Intl. above a cancelled* "*and*")]. Since I am now unable [*to make the payment which is I believe due, and shall be un-able (Intl.)*)] to fulfil[*l*] the engagements hereafter to mature; therefore the sooner the case is disposed of the better. Please write to my Brother for me in such terms as you can well understand I would use if allowed to write to him myself.

In like manner please write to my Sisters[4]. I asked Jeff. V.[5] when he & I parted, to join you as soon as he could and to remain with you; he could render you much assistance as well by his intelligence as his discretion: Have you heard from him? The servant reported by the newspapers to be with the children in New York, is I suppose Robert, indeed so hope.

Ellen came ashore, and it must have embarrassed you greatly under the circumstances to lose her before you could get another. Jim.[6] reported here that he knew where we had buried a large sum of gold at or near Macon[7]. This I heard after he had gone and in such manner as created the impression that he had gone on the same ship with you. The ready conclusion was that he had returned with assurances of zeal and fidelity [*to you and expecting (Intl.)*)] to find an opportunity [*an extra "to" is cancelled*] to rob your trunks [*here an "and" is cancelled, the period and capitol "T" are added*]. This greatly disturbed me until I found that he had gone by way of Raleigh[8]. Then remembering his complaint that he was not [*to be (Intl.)*)] furnished with transportation from here; another explanation of his fiction was afforded more creditable at least to his cunning. I have the prayer book[9] you sent, but the memorandum placed in it was witheld [*sic*]. The suit of dark grey clothes has also been received. It was like you in moments of such discomfort and annoyance as th[*ose (written over an erasure*)] to which you were subjected, to be careful about my contingent and future wants. Some day I hope to be able to tell you how in the long, weary hours of my confinement, busy memory has brought many tributes to your tender and ardent affection. The confidence in the shield of Innocence with which I tried to quiet your apprehensions and to dry your tears at our parting, sustains me still. If your fears have proved more prophetic than my hopes, yet do not despond— "Tarry thou the Lord's leisure; be strong, and He will comfort thy heart"[10]. Every day twice or oftener I repeat the prayer of St. Chrysostom[11] and assemble you all, each separately noted, on the right is Winnie, then Polly, Big-boy, Billie, then L.P. held by Aunty, and sometimes, as affection numbers the line, "the Little man" is found between his Brothers.[12] x x x x x _ _ _ _ _.

I daily repeat the hymn I last heard you sing, "guide me"[13] etc. It is doubly dear to me for that association. The one which follows it in our Book of common prayer[14] is also often present to me. It is a most beautiful lesson of humility & benevolence.

I have had here fresh occasion to realize the kindness of my fellow man. To the Surgeon and the Regtal.[15] [*both titles written over erasures*] Chaplain I am under many obligations. The officers of the Guard and of the Day have shown me increased consideration, such as their orders would permit. The unjust accusations which have been made against me in the newspapers of the day might well have created prejudices against me. I have had no opportunity to refute them by proof nor have I sought to do so by [*"such" crossed out*] statements of chronological and other easily to be verified facts which I might perhaps have been [*induced to make under other circumstances*; (*all but "to make" heavily written over erasures*)] & can therefore only attribute the perceptible change to those good influences which are always at work to confound evil designs. Be not alarmed by speculative reports concerning my condition. You can rely on my fortitude, and God has given me much of resignation to His blessed [*marred by ink blot*] will.

If it be His pleasure to reunite us, you will I trust find that His Fatherly correction has been sanctified to me, and that even in exile and obscurity I should be content to live unknown, quietly to labor for the support of my family; and thus to convince those who have misjudged me, that self seeking and ill regulated ambition are not elements of my character. Men are apt to be verbose when they speak of themselves and suffering has a rare power to develop selfishness; so I have wandered from the subject on which I proposed to write and have dwelt upon a person whose company I have for some time past kept so exclusively that it must be strange if he has not become tiresome.

Under the necessity before stated, and during our separation, you will have temporarily to select a place of abode where you will not be wounded by unkind allusions to myself, where you will have proper schools for the children and such social tone, moral and intellectual, as will best conduce to their culture. As well for yourself as for them you should endeavor to find a healthy location. To you a cold climate has been most beneficial, such also will best serve to strengthen the constitution of the children; and though the mind may hold mastery over the body, yet a strong frame is a great advantage to a student, and still more to him who in the busy world is called upon to apply his knowledge. If the news gatherer has rightly concluded that the children were on their way to Canada, I suppose it must have been under some intermediate arrangement. You will sufficiently understand the necessity for your presence with them and you must not allow your affectionate solicitude for me to interfere with your care for them.

It has been reported in the news papers that you had applied for permission to visit me in my confinement; if you had been allowed to do so the visit would have caused you disappointment at the time, and bitter memories afterwards. You would not have been allowed to hold private conversation with me and if we are permitted to correspond freely in relation to personal matters, not connected with public affairs, it will be a great consolation, and with it I recommend you to be content.

Your stay in Savannah[16] has been prolonged much beyond my expectation and I fear beyond your comfort. I do not know whether you are still there, but hope your whereabouts may be known at Washington and will ask that this letter may there receive the proper address.

Have the articles belonging to you personally and which were seized at the time of our capture been restored? You are aware that I have had no opportunity to present the case, and therefore you have had the unusual task of attending to it yourself. Money derived from the sale of your jewelry and the horses presented to you by Gentlemen of Richmond[17] could hardly be put on the same footing with my private property, and as little could they be regarded as public property, the proper subject of capture in war. The Heads of Executive Departments accustomed to consider questions of law and of fact, would I supposed take a different view of the transaction from subaltern officers of the Army _ _ _.

You will realize the necessity of extreme caution in regard to our correspondence. The quid nuncs if they hear you have received a letter from me will no doubt seek to extract something for their pursuit, and your experience has taught you how little material serves to spin their web.

Have you been sick? On the 21st of July little Maggie appeared to me in a most vivid dream, warning me not to wake you etc. etc. You know how little I have been accustomed to regard like things. Here such visions have been frequent, nor have they always been without comfort.

I am reluctant to close this first letter to you after so long an interval; but am warned that I may be abusing a privilege, as what I write is to be read by those to whom the labor will not be relieved by the interest which will support you.

If my dear Margaret is with you give to her my tenderest love, she always appears to me associated with little Winnie. Kiss the Baby for me, may her sunny face never be clouded, though dark the morning of her life has been.

My dear Wife, equally the centre of my love and confidence, remember how good the Lord has always been to me, how often He has wonderfully preserved me, and put thy trust in Him.

Farewell, may He who tempers the wind to the shorn lamb[18] whose most glorious attribute is mercy, guide and protect and provide for my distressed family; and give to them and to me that grace which shall lead us all to final rest in the mansions where there is peace that passeth understanding.[19]

Once more farewell, Ever affectionately

your Husband

Jeffn ~ .. Davis

Letter 2
(September 15, 1865)

Fortress Monroe Va.
15 Sept. 65

Varina Davis
My dear Wife

I wrote to you on the 21st Ulto.[1] and have anxiously expected an answer until so much time has elapsed that I have come to the conclusion that you did not receive my letter. It was sent as required via Washington D.C. to be inspected by the Atty. Genl. who was requested to ascertain your address and forward it. Genl. Miles[2] had previously at my request inquired, by telegraph, whether you were still in Savanna, but received no reply. You can readily imagine the painful solicitude I have felt and feel concerning you and our children. From Newspapers it appears that the three older children have been with your Ma. in Montreal and that they have left there, whither, not stated. In my former letter you were reminded of the importance of your presence with the children and urged not to allow your care for me to prevent you from going with them to some suitable place for them and for you.

I am so ignorant of all which has happened since we were separated, as to be unable to say more than you can anticipate, and apply according to your circumstances. When it shall be in my power to rejoin you we can make more permanent arrangements as the course of events and my condition may then indicate. Should my physical ability be not less than heretofore I feel that we shall be able to make our way in that mode of life to which we have both looked forward with hope; desiring quiet more, and shrinking from poverty less, than those good friends supposed to be possible, who so often sought to turn away the consequences of the loss of our property. I will not distress you by present reflections on a future of which too little can be foreseen to make its consideration useful. It is enough now to suggest that as your means may permit, you seek some healthy location where the children may have the advantage of proper schools and be surrounded by desirable social and moral influences; and where both you and they may be free from annoyance by those scavengers to a depraved appetite for abuse not of myself only, but of my family also. As only an occasional news paper is given to me I cannot know whether any replies are made to the fictions published in regard to myself; as their effect is not merely to prejudice public opinion against myself but extends likewise to those who were politically associated with me, it would not seem probable that even the timidity of this day would keep silent all, whose justification is the truth.

However this may be, you would be happier

away from such influences and the children will be safer under your supervision. If I can receive frequent letters from you, can have the fears for your health and safety, which so often oppress me, removed by direct information from you, it will be to me the consolation next to that of your presence. This last cannot be had, and if it were permitted we should not accept the indulgence at the cost in which it would be involved. Remember, when you write, that I am ignorant of all which has occurred to you since we were so suddenly separated, and give me such facts as will put me au courant[3] with events, and then I can better understand purposes and write more satisfactorily of family affairs.

In dreams you have lately come to me often in my prayers [sic] you and the children form a little group, spiritually, assembled in Our Heavenly Father's name, from whom I ask what in His wisdom it may be expedient[4] for us to have. It is a painful pleasure thus to summon you one by one and place you on memory's canvass [sic] grouped before me. The terms "painful" and "pleasure" are in contradiction, yet they are voluntarily made to coexist in many of the sorrowful trials of our life. Is Margaret with you, my imagination always connects her with little Winnie. Lest you should not have received my previous letter I renew the request that you will write to my Brother for me, and say to him what you will readily understand I would, if permitted to write to him. From my boyhood he stood to me in loco parentis[5], in after years he was to me the nearest friend and best advisor. Please also to write to my Sisters as you will know how, and explain the silence on my part there also. Do you know what has become of Sam, and his squad. If he comes to you for ad-

vice tell him to take his party back and join "old
Uncle Bob" and stay with him. If he has not been
interfered with the "old man" no doubt has kept
at least his church members together. Brother
Joe can direct in regard to matters of a business
nature. The heirs of Smith will probably come to
him. The land remains, everything else I understand was destroyed or removed. No deed was
made, the money remaining to be paid I have now
no power to raise, the best, indeed the only thing
I see to be done is to take back the land, and so it
would be well to inform the heirs. All incomplete
transactions had better be cancelled, as the only
means which I possessed when they were entered
into have been destroyed, and it only is possible to
meet the moral obligation.

[*First two words crossed out*] played a sharp trick
here for transportation I suppose, but of which I
gave you an account in my former letter, if you
don't get that I can repeat it in a future one.

I am sorry that you should have been alarmed
by reports in regard to my health. Those who utter
them can have no accurate information and are
never to be relied on. They have usually reported
the reverse of the fact and never the fact exactly. I
had fallen into a low condition the natural consequence of my situation; and had carbuncle on the
thigh and erysipelas in the nose, the former was
slow and painful, the latter was arrested before as-
cending to the eye, it reappeared and was arrested
as before. There was great physical prostration as
usual in such cases, and some fears that the disease
would extend to the brain; that apprehension however soon passed away, but while it existed may
have transpired[6] and given rise to the report which
has caused your alarm. The inflame[m]ation in the

nose at last assumed the type of the affection you may recollect I had in New Orleans and has now entirely disappeared. The Surgeon who attends me is both kind and skillful. I am deeply indebted to him and can assure you that while I am under his charge you need have no apprehension that any thing which is needful will be wanting.

During my confinement here I have marked a steady growth of that kindness on the part of the officers which my position rendered it proper for them to show: and so much depends upon the manner with which an unpleasant thing is done, that I find both in the absolute improvements which have been made in my treatment, and in the manner of doing the same thing, material relief.

Tell me when you write whether your personal property seized by the command which captured us has been restored. I expected Genls. Johnston and Sherman would regard the expedition as contrary to their agreement and take corresponding action, which would at least bear on the question of property claimed as capture of War.[7] If they or either of them have done so the fact has not become known to me. Genl. Sherman however I observe indignantly repels the idea of my having had specie enough to buy him, at the same time declining to state his price. All I can say on the point is that if he was to bring more than Beadle Bumble did I could not have made the purchase[8]. Who is meant by the "Brother in law of Jeff Davis" said to have been knocked down &c. &c. at Savannah? Is it all fiction?[9]

Have you heard from J. R. Davis? I know nothing of him since the surrender at Appomatox C H, but suppose he was paroled to go home.[10]

I hope soon to hear from you and to know

of all which concerns you and which has been by day and by night the subject of my thoughts. How is P.C.? Her bright little face is ever before me and I thank God that she is unconscious of all which distresses those nearest to her. Endeavor to be cheerful and hopeful. Have confidence in my ability to resist both physical and mental burthens[11], under the supporting grace of our Heavenly Father, who sends His comfort to alleviate every affliction. Let us accept His dispensation as that which is best, though our blindness should not be able to perceive the good designed, and thus we can with patience and resignation meet whatever fate is decreed to us. I cannot write to you as often as I would, a special permission is each time required and the requisite materials are furnished for that occasion only. There may be further relaxation, let us hope so, while the best use is made of present privileges.

Farewell, my loved Wife, remember that you cannot diminish my griefs by sharing them and strive to preserve the tone both of your mind and body by cultivating cheerful views of all things and charitable feelings towards all men. Kiss my Baby. God bless and guide you, and (if He will) restore us to each other in this world, ever prays your Husband

Jeffn. Davis

Letter 3
(September 26, 1865)

Fortress Monroe Va.
26 Sept. 1865

My dear Wife

Your much wished for letter of the 14th Inst.[1]
reached me yesterday and to day I have been furnished with writing materials to enable me to reply.
Your well known and beloved hand brought comfort to me before the envelop was broken. The spirit
which attends me waking and sleeping seemed to
be brought more into a real presence. Your letter
informs me of much which you did not intend to
communicate. I hope you are better now than when
you wrote, as the weather must be less oppressive.
One of the causes of my anxiety that you should
go with the children was the expectation that your
health would suffer if you remained in that hot,
crowded, and to you strange place. The assurance
given on the *Clyde* that you were no longer under
restraint, though it was modified when therefore I
proposed that you should leave that ship and take

passage on one bound to a northern port, still left
me under the belief that when you reached Savannah you would be free to go elsewhere, and I have
been always led to suppose that your stay there
was voluntary. Though not so related, the logic of
events leads to the conclusion that you too have
been a prisoner. Your inquiry by telegraph was
answered by Genl. Miles and from him I learned
at the same time that your address was Augusta,[2]:
I hope his dispatch reached you and relieved your
anxiety in regard to my health. My letter to you
written at that time gave you so full an account
of my disease that it will not be necessary in this
to notice it further than to say, that though it has
reappeared in a modified form there is no cause
for apprehension. My kind Physician, called in
the Chief Medical Director, who recently visited
this Post, and the result of their consultation was
that change to better quarters should be recommended. If their recommendation should secure
to me a purer and drier atmosphere I think there
will be a prompt and material improvement in my
health. But as I have said to you heretofore have
confidence in my ability to bear much and to bear
long, above all be not disturbed by the unwar-
ranted statements of those newsgatherers who
would earn their living by coining the tears of the
afflicted. Such people if they are here, have no
access to me, and can have no reliable information; if to make themselves acceptable to their
employers they invent stories painful to you, remember the motive and apply it as a test. It is true
that I did not wish you to know entirely the rigors
of my imprisonment and regret that you should
have learned them; it is true that my strength has
greatly failed me, and the loss of sleep has created

a morbid excitability; but an unseen hand has sustained me and a peace which the world could not give, and has not been able to destroy, will I trust uphold me to meet with resignation whatever may befal[*l*] me.

You do not mention Margaret and by saying your Ma. has not written to inform you about the Children, it is to be inferred that Marga. did not go with them. Your praise of Robert[3] is very grateful to me, I felt sure of him when giving him a parting charge. That which seems in him to be bad temper is rather a spirit of independence, an uncourtly virtue but in time of trial, a better reliance than submissive compliance. I am glad that Billy is his favorite not only because he is most helpless, but also because I am haunted by the suspicion that Betsy treated him harshly when an infant and I thought I saw the effect upon him afterwards. When he is numbered in the little group of prayer, my heart usually starts convulsively as though he appealed to me for protection. I have not heard of MyEllen, but she might be very near without my knowing it, and this, however desirous she might be to serve. Catherine no doubt repented and if she could control her angry passions would be better; but that is improbable, and when angry she is as little to be trusted as an insane person.[4] With you however, I rejoice in the truth and faithfulness of these humble friends: it is to your kindness and justice the best tribute which could be offered. It was similar manifestation on the part of the negroes at home that has caused me to feel so anxious for their welfare. Had they been willing to leave us and have done so without coercion it would have caused me for [*sic*] less regret. I should then have reckoned them greater losers by the change than ourselves. Their honesty will I trust be duly rewarded here and hereafter.

This is not the first time that we have found our humblest friends, the truest when no longer selfishly prompted. Yet I would not ascribe the defections of the higher class so much to treachery and deceit, as to timidity and avarice. Wishing to be relieved of responsibility for the past they offer in proof either of their little identification with the cause of the Confederacy or of their repentance for such connection; their censure, their accusation or their avowed hostility to the man on whom they lately conferred the highest office in their representative government, and who by performing the duties of that station has been rendered the object of special vengeance. If one is to answer for all upon him it most naturally and properly falls. If I alone could bear all the suffering of the country and relieve it from further calamity, I trust our Heavenly Father would give me strength to be a willing sacrifice; and if in a lower degree some of those who called me (I being then absent) to perform their behests, shall throw on me the whole responsibility; let us rejoice at least in their escape, expecting for them a returning sense of justice, when the stumbling blocks of fear and selfishness shall have been removed from their path.

In any event we have the satisfactory evidence that the class referred to is but a small portion of the people. The great mass accepting the present condition of affairs as the result of the War, and directing their attention to the future issues which are involved in the changes produced, would bury the inevitable past with the sorrow which is unmingled with shame.

As in my former letters I can only say that I have no information as to the purpose of the authorities in regard to myself. Neither as to accusation or proceeding.

I thank you for attention to my Brother, and grieve that it is not in my power to serve him. Gladly would I labor for him. There can I suppose be no question as to the restoration of his land. He did not leave home to enter the Service of the Confederacy, neither was the place abandoned. Persons were left in charge at each of the three quarters[5], and if they did not retain possession and cultivate some crop, it must have been because they were dispossessed by force. I refer to the River lands.[6] The amount of cotton which is promised on those places could have been easily produced without destroying the lawns. But will it be gathered? If my Brother would get some competent agent to attend to the division of the land and the receipt of rents, the place should yield a revenue sufficient to support him in comfort at some more agreeable residence than that will hereafter be. I hope you will soon have definite information as to the children, winter is approaching and they are in a very cold climate. Dear little P.C.: it is hard for me to realize that she has names for people. It must be a severe trial for her to teeth[e] in a hot climate and crowded as you must have been in Savnh. God grant that she may pass through the ordeal. Kiss her for one who loves her dearly though she does not know who he is. I did not doubt that your friends in Richmond would follow you with their prayers, and am glad that so many wrote to you. What became of Mrs. O'Melia[7] and how did she do?

Our kind neighbors sent me some time since

a bunch of cigars and a bottle of brandy. A reminder of the big glass of julep. Dr. Simmons who
you may recollect as a Surgeon in the old Army,
a friend of Dr. Wood, son in law of Mr. Giddings
of Balto is now Medical Inspector of this Dept.
& is stationed at Richd.[8] He was here some time
since and I have cause to be thankful to him for
subsequent kindness. My little friend[9] who has so
kindly attended to sending my meals and looking
after my clothes when sent to wash, has gone to
the Moravian school near to Easton. I requested
her Father to let Mary Jane[10] know of her. She
used to ride on horseback and in my daily walk I
sometimes saw her. If I had known how to get it, I
would have given your fine saddle to her.

My dear Winnie I felt how anxious you would
be to be with me if you knew that I was sick and
in pain. Need I say that every pang reminded me
how often your soft touch and loving words have
soothed me in like times of suffering. How sadly I
felt that public cares and frequent absence and pre-
occupation with disagreeable subjects had prevented me from making even the poor return which it
was in my power to give. That time so long looked
for when we should be apart from the world, and
quietly occupied with objects of common interest
to us, seemed to rise before me like the "convenient
season" of the impenitent. I have prayed if it be the
will of our Father that it might yet be given to me
to show you how much and how truly I am your's,
and with such poor measure as I could mete to
return when you were sick your services in kind.
My good Wife, the Lord will care for you, there
always seems to me to be an assuring answer when
I pray especially for you. The needy and the sorrow stricken who have been relieved and soothed

by you, smooth your way to the favor of Him who shows mercy to the merciful. My heart is sustained by the conviction that we shall meet again in this world, that even before human judgement my innocence of wrong to my fellow man will prevail, though many seek my destruction. The bigotry which gave power to false witnesses and frightened truth from the presence of the Judges, though it lives, no longer reigns. Be hopeful and again I say "tarry thou the Lord's leisure."

May the Lord guide and comfort you, ever prays with all the fervor of devoted affection your Husband.

Jeffn ~.. Davis

Mrs. Varina Davis, near Augusta, Ga.

[*Written longways on page 1, left side*:] P.S. I met Mr. Clay in our walk, he asked me to give his love to you and the children. He is now in better health, but is much changed. Hair and beard quite grey. Jno Mitchell is here.[11] I saw him in like manner. He looks thin and feeble, is said to be consumptive. We are not allowed to visit each other or to converse when we meet in the open air. When Mr. Clay was quite sick I earnestly desired to be with him.

D.

Letter 4
(October 11-12, 1865)

Fortress Monroe Va.
11ᵗʰ Oct. 1865

My dear Wife,

To day I have had the good fortune to receive yours of the 22ⁿᵈ Ulto. being the second letter since we parted. The former one was of the 14ᵗʰ Ulto. and was answered on the 26ᵗʰ. I write as often as I can and hope the three letters heretofore sent will all reach you, as the delays consequent on the manner of transmission will permit. Though I have little cheering to communicate it is as great a pleasure to me to write to you, as it is for you to hear from me. You mustn't allow yourself to be distressed by dwelling on my suffering when sick and deprived of the consolation of your presence. I have tried and not without success to possess my soul in patience.[1] A varied life has given me experience in most forms of trial. When a Cadet I lay for more than four months in Hospital[2] and rarely saw any one save when it was thought I was about to die, then some of my friends were allowed to stay with me at night. I should have more resources to sustain me now than then, and as much fortitude as when you have seen me suffer.

The report you saw of my change of quarters was not true, but that which had not then been determined has since occurred. On the second of this month I was removed to a room on the second floor of a house built for officers quarters. The dry air, good water and a fire when requisite have already improved my physical condition and with increasing strength all the disturbances due to a low vitality it is to be expected will disappear, as rapidly as has been usual with me after becoming convalescent. I am deeply indebted to my attending Physician who has been to me much more than that term usually conveys. In all my times of trouble, new evidences have been given to me of God's merciful love and of the goodness of the human heart. This always more and more impresses me with the amount of my omitting and committing sinfulness and the immeasureable [*sic*] debt of gratitude which is due to Him who gives everything to us, and only requires that we shall properly use them. From such manifestations I also desire charity for those in whom humanity is obscured by ignorance or malice. As only that which is true is permanent; on this humanity of the unbiassed heart and on that sense of justice which I believe to be general, however partial may be the perception of what is just, is based my continuing hope of the better things to come, though I may not behold them, still may I hope that they are coming.

You have no doubt observed that beautiful letter written by Ladies of Holly Springs[3] to Presdt. Johnson, on my behalf. It was the more valuable to me because I had not seen them during the war, and had not had it in my power to give any additional proof of my care for that section of country. No region suffered more, yet they have continued to feel for me as I have for them. You have I suppose also seen that the Bar of Mississippi have a committee who have tendered their services for my defence. They were not selected for political affinity, but one of them who was my consistent opponent is from our former contests only the better able to appreciate my creed and motives. I have referred to these as tokens which may relieve your anguish by showing that those for whose cause I suffer are not unworthy of the devotion of all which I had to give.

I do not know whether Brother Joe has gone to the Hurricane or not.[4] A newspaper paragraph states that his property has been restored, though the accuracy of the description was marred by adding that he had been in the army[5], yet it was still unusually near to the truth for a paragraph which included my name, to have but one misstatement connected with it. As I wrote to you his right to the comparatively little which remains can hardly be controverted.

By your reference to Cousin Joe. Smith[6] I suppose he must have visited you. There is no one who would be more willing to serve you and few better suited by character to do so agreeably [sic]. Watson[7] has probably pressed his credit boldly in Tobacco purchases and thus led to the conclusion that he had grown rich. It will be fortunate for him if it does not entirely fail; though enough of luck may make him what he is reported to be. This is however merely a supposition on my part founded on his former pursuits and the facts contained in your letter. Do you know whether Mary Jane has changed her residence? Is William[8] still in Augusta? As I can write to none of the family except yourself you will understand that all which concerns them is to me unknown. "The Herald"[9] claims to give me regular information concerning my family, but if it did contain such news, as I only get occasionally a copy, the promise would not be fulfilled.

From the published speech of Genl. Slocum I infer the "freedmen" in Mississippi are doing better than in the state of your involuntary sojourn. See Herald of the 5th Inst.

Did Jeff leave his writing "behind". And why don't Polly write to you? Has Margaret gone to join the children, I agree with you that her presence is desirable especially during your absence, yet she has during my confinement been to me a dream inseparable from Pei [sic]. I cannot realize that the baby walks and talks however imperfectly. Kiss her for honoring me with the first fruit of her putting her hand to paper. You cannot hear but may feel how gratified I am by the receipt of the Photographs. Guillaume's apology does not apply, the principal figure "est sacrifieé".[10] But it is all in all to me. "For weel ken I my ain lassie" etc. etc. you know the rest.[11] Your letter gave me the first information in regard to Mildred and her family.[12] Her first Brother is equal to any fortune, and worthy of a good one. The little I see and hear indicates that it is the policy of Presdt. Johnson to restore property in most cases to those who have been deprived of it, and I hope these will not belong to the excluded class. There is however in all such cases that consolation which an approving conscience gives, and with which any personal deprivation becomes tolerable. I have lately read the "Suffering Saviour"[13] by the Revd. Dr. Krum[m]acher and was deeply impressed with the dignity, the sublime patience of the model of christianity[14] as contrasted with the brutal vindictiveness of unregenerate man; and with the similitude of the portrait given of the Jews to the fierce prosecutions which pursued the Revolutionists[15] after the restoration of the Stuarts. One is led to ask did Sir Hy. Vane and the Duke of Argyle[16] imitate the more than human virtue of our Saviour[17] or was their conduct the inspiration of a conscience void of offence in that whereof they were accused.

I do not know personally either the officers from whom you received wanton annoyance or him by whom you were relieved, and had hoped that in this age of boasted civilization, that indignities designed to degrade a cause by making it's agents appear as the "vilest of mankind,"[18] would not have been applied to my helpless and unoffending Wife. Like you however I can only pray, but my faith in the supremacy of justice assures me that they both will have their reward.

Oct. 12th I was not able, on yesterday, to obtain an envelop and therefore postponed the conclusion of my letter until this morning. If you see Mr. & Mrs. Burt[19] present me to them most kindly. Also make my grateful acknowledgements to Mr. Schley for his kindness to you.[20]

Again I thank you for the Photographs. Little Winnie appears to me better in that in which she is taken with you. The photograph after [*Neke?*] I wear next to my heart, this is placed with it. You have changed much, that I could anticipate, but I complain of your sad expression. Be not downcast. We must meet cheerfully whatever affliction it may be God's will we should bear. Misfortune should not depress us, as it is only crime which can degrade. Beyond this world there is a sure retreat for the oppressed; and posterity justifies the memory of those who fall unjustly. To our purblind view there is much which is wrong, but to deny that in the great scale of wordly affairs every event tends to what is right, is to question the wisdom of Providence or the existence of the mediatorial government.

I hope when you next write that you will be able to give me news of the children. How they are, where they are and what they are doing. The want of information and my extreme anxiety concerning them, unfit me to make any additional suggestions in regard to them. To the protection of our Heavenly Father I commend both them and you, praying that He will guard you all from any evil to which you may be exposed. If I were a believer in dreams my days would be spent in reviewing the visions of the night. In the broken sleep which I get, you and the children frequently visit me and generally I am happy to say with more pleasing aspect than in my wakeful reflections. Little Polly comes oftenest and usually with the gentle, thoughtful air of a woman. You have not mentioned in your letters my saintly and beloved Sister Lucinda.[21] Do you hear from her? Jos. Smith[22] if you saw him must have told you all about the family.

I am not allowed intercourse with Mr. Clay but see him occasionally when we walk in the open air. He is now better I think than when he came here, and looks much more cheerful than he did a short time ago. As he is generaly less restricted than myself, I take it for granted that he is allowed equal or greater freedom in writing to his Wife, but it might be a comfort to her to learn the opinion of another in regard to his health.

The baby's mode of speech is the method of nature. The like is found in all languages which were spoken long before they were written. It has been regarded as one of the beauties of the Greek. I found it still more prominent in the Chippewa.[23] By great freedom of abridgement a single word is formed out of many, and expresses the agent & his condition, the object, the action and it's effect. It is termed "<u>polysynthetic</u>".

Though my letter is long I am reluctant to stop. If I were allowed writing material it would be a pleasant occupation to give you daily my thoughts with a record of the few events which mark my prison life. But it is perhaps well, as having nothing with which to keep even the notes one would make in reading a book, and with a desire to forget what is painful, many things are lost which it would be worse than useless to preserve.

I am as ignorant as heretofore of the purpose of the authorities in regard to me. My counsel has not visited me. The few newspapers I see still manifest what appears to me an unaccountable hostility, and a strange degree of ignorance or recklessness in their statements in regard to my public career. Enough however is known by many to secure sooner or later a refutation at least of such slanders as affect those whom I represented. Being powerless to direct the current, I can only wait to see whither it runs.

We have had a few cold days here, but the weather is now pleasant. The trees as [*sic*] still covered with leaves, but they are assuming the hue of autumn. The feeling of cold carries my thoughts to the children in Canada, but I am consoled by the confidence that they will not be neglected; and then to "Old Uncle Bob" in Missi. Who will take our place in regard to him, and the "old people" who were with him? Farewell my dear Wife, ever trusting in the

[*Beginning here, JD wrote the rest of this letter at the top of his first page, at right angles to the previous writing, but mostly in empty space above the dateline.*]

The [*sic*] mercy of God, I prayerfully hope that we shall be reunited in this world, but humbly strive with becoming resignation to say, Father thy will be done. There is now no reason to suppose that my imprisonment will so impair my health as soon to terminate my life. Every development of truth must diminish the desire to punish me, and therefore there is reasonable ground for hopefulness. Let us trust in Him whose wisdom cannot err and whose power cannot fail to effect His will. More now depends on you than at any former time; to be equal to the trial you require sana mens in sana corpore[24], therefore cherish hope and cultivate cheerfulness as conducive thereto.

Once more my love, farewell. Through my prison bars my free spirit flies to and hovers around you. Daily and nightly my prayers are offered for you, and there is a peace which tells me they are heard. May God be with you. Again dearest and yet again farewell.

Ever affectionately yr. Husband

Jeffn. Davis

Letter 5
(October 20, 1865)

Ft. Monroe, 20th Oct. 65

Mrs. Varina Davis
My dear Wife

Yesterday brought me your letters of Sept. 4 and Oct. 1 with note of Oct. 2. And enclosures, viz. Letter from Ellen, one from Jeff., and circular of the Academy at Sault au Recollet. Though the tones could not be those employed in happier hours, they were consolatory to me and relieved many of my distressing anxieties. You of course understood that in the absence of the requisite data I did not intend on former occasions to do more than suggest what would be preferable if no impediment existed. Not imagining that you would be restricted to a place which I had stated was objectionable on account of the evil effect which the climate would produce, and in which you would be an entire stranger, I only felt the hardship of your being required to go there; and feeling that your constant care was needful to our small children I expressed the wish that you would

go with them to some place where they and you
would be more advantageously situated. You have
done what seems to me the best under the circumstances and I trust God will so order all things as
to justify the action taken by it's future results.

Chafed by harsh restraints and agonized by
fears for me, it may have been naturally expected
that a nervous woman would give expression to
her feelings and seek to make her griefs known
to her Husband's friends. [*Papers of JD has "and"
here;* Jefferson Davis Essential Writings *does not*],
perhaps it was therefore that detectives were put
around you; and I am proud of your self denial,
and grateful that the sickness consequent has had
no worse effect upon you and your infant. We
should not be surprised that those whose palms
itch for gold should attribute to me a like vice, and
therefore may have hoped by watching you to find
hidden treasure. Newspapers publish silly accounts
of large sums of specie possessed by me and abandoned, of course every intelligent man knows that
my office did not make me the custodian of public
money, but such slanders impose on and serve to
inflame the ignorant, the very ignorant who don't
know how public money was kept and how drawn
out by the hands of those who were responsible
for it. My children as they grow up and prove the
pressure of poverty, must be taught the cause of it;
and I trust they will feel as I have, when remembering the fact that my Father was impoverished
by his losses in the War of the Revolution.

The religion we profess has this peculiar
characteristic, that just in proportion as we advance in preparation for the world to come, is our
happiness in this increased. Our injuries cease
to be grievous in proportion as Christian charity

enables us to forgive those who trespass against us, and to pray for our enemies. I rejoice in the sweet, sensitive nature of my little Maggie, but I would she could have been spared the knowledge which inspired her "grace" and the tears which followed it's utterance.[1] As none could share my suffering, and as those who loved me were powerless to diminish it, I greatly preferred that they should not know of it. Separated from my friends of this world, my Heavenly Father has drawn nearer to me, His goodness and my unworthiness are more sensibly felt, but this does not press me back, for the atoning Mediator is the way, and his hand upholds me.

I trust Maggie will be happy, her loving temper will suit the government of the Nuns, and they will probably soon become attached to each other. When I was a child the kindness of the Friars so won upon my affection that the impression has never been effaced, but has the rather extended from them to their whole church. Her letter to me has not arrived, nor has your's of Sept. 1st which you mention as having enclosed to be forwarded. The big boy has not improved much in his writing but the warm heart was not to be hidden or hushed by his want of skill clerkly. You have no doubt answered his inquiry but when you write to him again, tell him how glad I was to see his letter, how anxious I am that he should be a good boy and learn fast, how much I love him and how constantly I pray for him. Where is Robert? Would he not be more useful to you under the present condition of the family than elsewhere. I hope your Ma. is comfortably situated and that she and Billy will get on well together, but unless he has a good nurse you know she will over work herself.

Give my love to her when you write and to Margaret who is I suppose there. You will know how to express my feelings for both of them.

Joe. D & S[2] have not disappointed and if you should hereafter require the services of either of them they will no doubt come as fully at your command as when they recently came to you unbidden. Please write to Ellen for me thank her for the kind true hearted letter she wrote to me. It is in the spirit I honor and expected from her, may she never be shaken in her confidence in the supremacy of justice and the protecting power of innocence. Little Winnie in the photograph grows more like herself than she seemed when it first came. My Winnie's sadness continues. May a brighter sun lighten her heart and enliven her picture.

William's conduct surprises me. I will only say of it that it was unlike either his Father or his Mother, and of him that I wish never to hear of him again. I am sorry you did not see Sam.; when he joins "old Bob" there will be supplied to him the only thing he needs, judgement. Tom & Charley expressed to you what is I believe the feeling of all our family negroes. I hope their fidelity will be duly rewarded and regret that we are not in a situation to aid and protect them. There is I observe a controversy which I regret as to allowing negroes to testify in court. From Brother Joe, many years ago, I derived the opinion that they should be made competent witnesses, the jury judging of their credibility; out of my opinion on that point arose my difficulty with Mr. Cox, and any doubt which might have existed in my mind was removed at that time. The change of relation diminishing protection, must increase the necessity. Truth only is consistent, and they must be acute and well trained, who can so combine as to make falsehood appear like truth when closely examined. After full consideration I believe Jim innocent and that the story was the invention of a lower man having higher position.

I will try to get the commentaries of which you write. Would like to read the same books with you, but under present circumstances this would be difficult and objectionable. Difficult because I have little field for selection and objectionable because entertaining books, poetry and romance would excite, whereas my effort is to keep senti-ment subdued and to live in the region of driest fact, I would not have you reduced to the same fare, as mingling with the world the impressions of poetry and romance come as a relief and do not remain to injure.

Dear Le Pi's hair came safely and softly lies with me; you are now in that condition which is the symbol of occupation. May you soon have all your cares and objects of love about you again.

Brother Joe. should not I think return to the river place. All is changed, he will be troubled beyond his strength by the confusion which must exist, an Agent will suit the new regime much bet-ter than the old one. If he goes back why not take the Brierfield House. He can claim possession, as owner of the land. But my decided opinion is that in the existing condition neither he nor Lize should stay there. I cannot write to him.

The saddest effect which has been produced on me is in impaired memory. Accustomed to rely on it with confidence it is painfully embarass-ing [sic] to me, especially as to names and dates. In regard to events it is less felt and by associa-

tion only can I measure time. This year came in
on Sunday and thus the tables in the Prayer book
[*sic*] serve as a calendar. A circumstance to which I
am much indebted. Have you retained our family
Bible? If so the dates you ask for are there. 1859
& 1864 must be the years—The month of the first
was I think April & day 18th. the last was Satur-
day preceding the meeting of Congress__ I have
nothing to refer to in aid of memory. It was very
kind of these friends. Pardon me I cannot. * x x
x   For say, three months after I was imprisoned
here two hours of consecutive sleep were never
allowed to me,more recently it has not been so
bad, but it is still only broken sleep which I get at
night, and by day my attention is distracted by the
passing of the Sentinels who are kept around me
as well by day as by night. I have not sunk under
my trials, am better than a fortnight ago and trust
shall be sustained under any affliction which it
may [*be*] required of me to bear. My sight is affected but less than I would have supposed if it
had been foretold that a light was to be kept where
I was to sleep, and that I was at short intervals
to be aroused and the expanded pupils thus frequently subjected to the glare of a lamp. You have
repeated the request for a description of my situation and I have complied in part. Already regret
having done so and hope you will be satisfied of
the correctness of the rule heretofore observed.
Of my occupation a brief account will suffice. In
the morning as soon as dressed I read the morning prayer (family) sometimes adding a chapter of
the new Testament and a Psalm. After breakfast
read, at this time Bancroft's History of the United
States. Soon after read the morning service, on
Sundays, Wednesdays & Fridays, add the com-

munion service, the Collect, Epistle and Gospel
and the Litany.[3] In the afternoon read whatever
book occupies me and when Genl. Miles comes,
go out to walk say, for an hour on the parapet. In
the evening read the service as appointed. Family
prayers at night. To the morning & evening service
a modified form of the prayer for a person going
to sea and of the prayer for a person under affliction are always added[4]. of [sic] food I am quite
satisfactorily supplied by the Doctor's family, and
my appetite is to blame for any want of apprecia-
tion. My cot is now comfortable and I have plenty
of water and fire—do not imagine horrible things
and suffer vicariously for me. If President Johnson
ever finds out the exact state of the case, I think he
will remove the most disagreeable features in the
discipline and until then or some other change, be
assured I will bear it with the patience that lightens
burdens, and expect me to get better rather than
worse. There is soon to be a change of the garrison
here, I will be sorry to part from many of the officers—but as they are to go home I should rejoice
for such as are entitled to my gratitude. Au reste[5],
as I cannot control, so I may hope it will be for the
better.

I have not seen Jordan's critique[6] and am at
a loss to know where that game was played and
was lost by my interference. If the records are
preserved they dispose summarily of his romances
past, passing and to come. Be not distressed by the
conduct of those who willfully misrepresent, neither of the others whose timidity but not their will
consents. If those whom I have served turn against
me theirs is the shame, and time will make them
feel it. The events were of a public character and
it is not possible for men to shift their responsibil-

ity to another. Every one who has acted must have made mistakes, and the frank acknowledgement of his errors will be the best defence he can make to the public and the only one beneficial to his conscience. Let him who has changed his theory confess it, let him whose opinons are unchanged conform his action to the changed circumstances, and both classes may preserve their integrity and live and work in harmony. Our life is spent in choosing between evils. and he would be most unwise who would refuse the comparative good thus to be obtained. History is ever repeating itself, but the influence of Christianity and letters has softened its harsher features. The wail of the destitute woman and children who were left on the shore of Cork after the treaty of Limerick, still rings in the ears of all who love right and hate oppression; but bad as was the treatment of the Irish then, those scenes of which you were reading not long before you left Richmond, enacted by Philip of Spain in the low countries were worse. The unfortunate have always been deserted and betrayed; but did ever man have less to complain of when he had lost power to serve. The critics are noisy—perhaps they hope to enhance their wares by loud crying. The multitude are silent, why should they speak save to Him who hears best the words most secretly uttered. My own heart tells me the sympathy exists, that the prayers from the family hearth have not been hushed. Then be ye, not charitable, but loving and confiding still to those from whom I have received much more that I deserved and as you know far more of official honors that I desired.

Little Polly will I suppose resume French, the boy has probably forgotten much and will be almost a beginner. If the course of the school is to put boys early at Latin I would not object. It is the root of the languages of Southern Europe, and enters largely into the etimology [*sic*] of our own; but the argument for it's study most conclusive with me is that it is the best exercise for the mind of which a small boy is capable. Strange though it may seem I have generally found when a school boy, that those from warm countries would expose themselves most to cold and for a time at least would bear it best. It will be well that care should be taken to prevent our children from being thus injured. Some of our friends might get the little dog, especially if it's history is not known. Horrible you say, I answer generally true. The individual may be an exception of that I know nothing, though his reputation for gallantry is suggestive of generosity and humanity. I have asked for the Schomlerg Cotte family and Cumming, [*sic*] Scripture readings—The latter I hope the Chaplain may have. The Psalter and Lessons for the day will give us that daily reading in common which you suggest. It is not easy for me to know the hour except by the relieving of Sentinels—which is every two hours beginning at 9 A.M. When in the casement I constructed on the floor of the embrasure a partial dial, here it is not practicable. To me hours are alike, but to you these will be frequent occurrences, visitors, domestic employments etc, etc which will not leave you entire command of your time. When I read though you shall not be at the same time reading or praying with me, I will know you have been or will be uttering the same words, engaged with the same thoughts. There are other things of which I would write yet do not. The events in your letter are understood, I think thoroughly, but it would avail nothing to comment on them. It is generally true that complaint diminishes the capacity to bear, certainly it does the freedom of inquiry into the nature of the grievance.

It was not my intention to have entered on a third sheet yet I must stop before having written of many things affecting us all. Imprisonment in solitude gives much time for speculation, but in this rapidly changing current of events thoughts not having fresh data are little worth.

Kiss the Baby for me, may God grant to me the sight of you both, may he preserve you from all harm in this world and gives [*sic*] us all grace to meet in Heaven as we assemble specially in my prayers twice or oftener daily.

Farewell my dear Wife. You have a key to my heart and know its unuttered feelings. That God may remember us in mercy, and grant our petitions as His wisdom will provide ever prays with unchanging devotion your Husband

Mrs. Varina Davis   Jeffn Davis

Letter 6
(November 3-4, 1865)

Fortress Monroe Va. 3 Nov. 65

My dear Wife,

Your's of the 23ᵈ Ulto. received this day and brought the only cheering ray which ever lights up the gloom of my imprisonment. When I grow restless from desire to receive another letter from you I draw comfort from reperusal of those preserved. The letters written to you have acknowledged your's by their dates. Those not received may yet come to hand, the chances for delay being multiplied by the forms of transmission. I should have noticed the circular of the Convent, which was received with Boy's letter. Your account of the two schools was full, and upon it rested the satisfaction I expressed in a letter written a few days before the date of your's. That letter will have shown you, that the inquiries made in a former letter were answered by you in those received by me on the 19ᵗʰ Ulto. I heard recently that Brother Jos.[1] was in Washington D.C. It seemed to me improbable and I feared he

would unsuccessfully seek, if there, to visit me
and would not be well able to bear a refusal. I am
glad he did not undertake such a journey, that he
was not so near me and yet unable to see me, and
that he is with our family at the "old place". The
chances are against my seeing him again in this
world. There are many things I wish him to know
and if permitted would write to him, as without
full information he cannot well understand my
course in relation to the military operations in Ga.
& Ala.[2] about which you may recollect he made
some remarks. You know how much I have from
boyhood valued his good opinion, and he cannot
know how little I had to do with the series of blunders in that quarter, or the nature of the obstructions to any important success, however palpably
possible and expedient, however immediate and
pressing the necessity. My fate was not veiled by
such sanguine temperament as will not see the
precipice. If hope had not lighted the thorny path
of duty, conscience required that path should be
followed wherever the same might lead; and only
those who sinning from the beginning, in acting
from conformity and not faith; who therefore were
not under the rule of conscience, whose guide was
selfishness, were qualified to find and to follow
another road.

 I have been reading Bancroft's History of
the U States.[3] It is a work of great research and
marked by fairness and regard for accuracy. It was
to me most interesting by its marginal reference
to the books and pamphlets connected with his
subject, which I had read many years ago; thus as
it were peopling my prison with old acquaintance.
Things which I had learned only through tradition
are also presented on the basis of authentic record.

In many passages his style rises to the highest level
and through the whole runs undefiled the love of
of [*sic*] justice and liberty.

In his general description of puritanism as it
existed in the early settlements of New England, I
found justification for the letter I gave to the agent
for collecting funds to build a monument at Plym-
outh.

Neither the "Schomberg Cotte family [*sic*;
quotation not closed], nor Cummings scripture readings [*sic*] are to be had here. The library is mainly
composed of works on military subjects and the
text books used at the U.S. Military Academy.
The officers who were here being so likely at short
notice to change their station would properly avoid
the collection of books.

The anxious wish of our big boy to hear of
me and his recognition of the fact that he could
only do so indirectly are touching evidences of
his affection and growing thought. You will know
how to give to him, and to my sweet daughter,
their Father's love and unceasing solicitude. Billy's
bright and inquiring face is often, very often before
me. May God preserve and lead in ways of safety
and usefulness.

I am glad to hear of Mary P. of whom I
could expect only praise worthy thoughts and ac-
tions. Though the world judges by the test of success; the heart yields not to the judgement, and its
nobler impulses prompt the retributive justice that
follows wrong. __ I have read the Satires to which
you referred, and felt how little we can realize the
experience of another until we have felt the like
in our own persons. Were it otherwise how rapid
would be the progress of mankind both in mental
and moral culture, Each generation bequeathing

it's acquisition to the immediate use of the next.
When the prayer of King Solomon for wisdom
was answered by divine endowment, he sought
to enrich his Son by it as an inheritance. Into few
pages the stores of his knowledge were concentrated; but could he thus "give subtilty to the simple,
to the young man knowledge and discretion? [*no
end quotation marks*].

[*This sentence is squeezed in at the top of the
page in very tiny script:*] Your renewed request for a
description of my room & account of my clothes
is noted. [(*Intl.*) *Gen. Miles would not send the one he
wrote.*]

Jno. Mitchell has been released. He was permitted [*to*] take leave of me through the grates and
offered to write to you. His health suffered by his
imprisonment here and I fear his lungs are diseased. Our friend Clay is not well recently. I have
not seen him for some time, not having been out to
walk lately, on account of a series of boils or a carbuncle with a succession of points which rose in
my right arm pit and which has prevented me from
putting on my coat since the day after I last wrote
to you until a few days back. The disease is now
probably at an end, but rains have prevented me
from going out since I have been able to do so. The
chaplain who has kindly aided me in the matter
of religious books leaves with the Regt.[4] which is
now about to be mustered out of service. Though
he has not been able to visit me often his departure
is to me a matter of regret. Though quite young,
his discretion and information in his profession
are large, and his pious zeal noticeable. He was a
School-fellow of the Laughlin boys[5] to whom he

referred affectionately. Florida's letters to them had been shown to him and from having heard of me through them he seemed from the first time we meet [*sic*] to feel an interest in me.

I perceive by the news papers that Mr. Seddon[6] has been in confinement and it is inferrable [*sic*] that he has been released. From the same source that Mr. Trenholm and Reagan have been released. This was most gratifying intelligence to me. I hope Mr. Mallory will soon have the same good fortune. They are of that class of men who following their honest convictions may always be relied on to the extent of their pledges, and each of them will be useful at home especially when so much confusion prevails.

The papers are sent to me irregularily [*sic*] the same papers not being furnished in series so that I sometimes see part of a matter only, if it be contained in separate numbers. I have too long and too earnestly watched public affairs to be able to dismiss the care, though I may realize my inability to promote the welfare of those in whose service so large a part of my life has been spent and towards whom I look with unchanging affection.

From an officer of the new garrison I have learned that our friends in Portland are so nearly in the condition we left them that time seems to have stood still for them. The only changes are, the death of Mr. Little, and the marriage of his widow, and the removal of Mr. McDonald. Our Landlady is in statu quo[7]. Miss Clapp is unmarried. The fine house opposite our window is unfinished etc. etc.

I have carefully read McCauley's [*sic*] History of England and not without disappointment. A better title for his work would have been Biography of William of Orange. The great movement [*in?*] England the reformation of the Monarchical system which rose on the downfall of feudalism, the exaltation of the people to the position of founder of states are subordinated to the purpose of making a pedestal for the statue of William the third. A dissenter could find in Cromwell's greatness an argument against the accusations with which loyalists sought to disgrace his memory; but like reasoning would have prevented the conclusion that Marlborough was guilty of the meanest vices of mankind. ___ It has been so long since I read the Iliad that its beauty remains to me indistinct, though the impression is yet enough to make all translations tame. The sound of the Greek is to Homer's verse a charm which no other language can borrow. Well read it might move the heart of one who did not know the meaning of a single word, and tell its general tale like the music of an opera.

Day by day the photograph of Pie grows on me in expressiveness. I had already found her like Sister Anne when your letter came describing her ways as I have found Sister A's[8] portrayed when she was a child. It is difficult for me to realize the baby is <u>walking and talking</u> and hard to think and be patient. I am sustained by a power I know not of. [*These last four words, though quite legible, begin a passage of seven and a half lines which were marked through as if for deletion. Respecting the wish for privacy, we press on and come to "the death of Lizzies's father."*] It will be a sad blow to her for she is worse off than a widow. If I were permitted to do so, would write to her, and though both may be little worth, would offer my sympathy and love. I have no means of communicating with anyone but you, and as I understand the orders, all communications to you must pass through Washington, and be viseèd [*sic*] This may account for any delay in the answers to your message to Genl. Miles. [(*Intl.*) *in very tiny script*]. Pie's silky lock [*of hair*], her separate photograph, Boy's letter and the view of Maggies [*sic*] school are together. Armistead[9] always was true gold and with peculiarities which might sometimes displease his Wife is a true hearted unwavering friend—I feel as it were mesmerically drawn to the lonely pair, and there are none to whom I would more securely trust. Sister Maran[10] has improved since you saw [*Intl.*] her—cheerfulness has followed change of association and more active occupation. Her Husband is a sincere, honest man and prudent when his friend's matter is his charge.

The cigars were received. And as they have been smoked your caution came too late. I took them in small doses and so no injury, but some good was the result. Do you know where your likeness by Dodge is? [*In following passage many words are too faint to read*:] Margaret will no doubt . . . of the children. In a former letter . . . your present inquiry as to my approval of the course taken by you in regard to them. John[11] will not forget them and his head and heart are alike sound. The field for your selection was so narrow that at least until you could go with them, no other plan was before you. You will have need to watch the tendency to political disturbance there. It appears to be the only practicable object of the Fenians, if present, for early movement . . . their purpose. I have no data I can merely make surmises[12] Jno. and Preston[13] can probably learn and advise.

4th Nov. Today is dark and wet, not cold, but chilly.

The trees in the fort are sheltered by the defenses well, but their leaves tell that summer has gone. I have nothing learned in regard to the purposes concerning myself. Counsel has not visited me, and the newspaper stories are so repugnant to the Constitution and the decisions under it, that they must have been made by the ignorant for the ignorant. [*A total of eight lines is here obliterated and in the left margin appears; "7th Nov. 65. J.D."*] I draw near the end of my paper and have the pang of this kind of parting, from my beloved and trusted.

What under Providence may be in store for us I have no ability to foresee. I have tried to do my duty to my fellow man and while my penitent prayers are offered to our heavenly Father for forgiveness of the sins committed against him, I have the sustaining belief that he is full of mercy; and knowing my inmost bent will acquit me where man, blind man seeks to condemn. From our mediating saviour I humbly trust to receive support, and whatever may befal[*l*] me in this world, to have justice, dictated by divine wisdom and tempered with divine mercy in the next. Be not then despondent but let us rather seek only so to live that we may not fear to die, looking with hope to the resurrection which we have by promise, and to the home where the weary shall be at rest, in the midst of joys not to be conceived of in our present state.

[*The following three paragraphs ending this letter are written crosswise at the top of the first page:*]

Kiss dear little Winnie for me and as she grows teach her how her Father loved her when she was too young to remember. Try to make my thanks to Mr. Schley and the Ladies equal to my gratitude. Did he not call on me when I was last in Augusta, or was it another of the family, I think it was he.

Farewell dear Wife my prayers go up constantly for you, your image is ever before me, my spirit is about you, and my faith tells me that our merciful Father will give us whatever it is expedient we should have.

You know what I would say at least what I always feel and suppressing utterance I say again Farwell/Dearest farewell.

Your Husband

Jeffn Davis

Mrs. Varina Davis,

Augusta,

Ga.

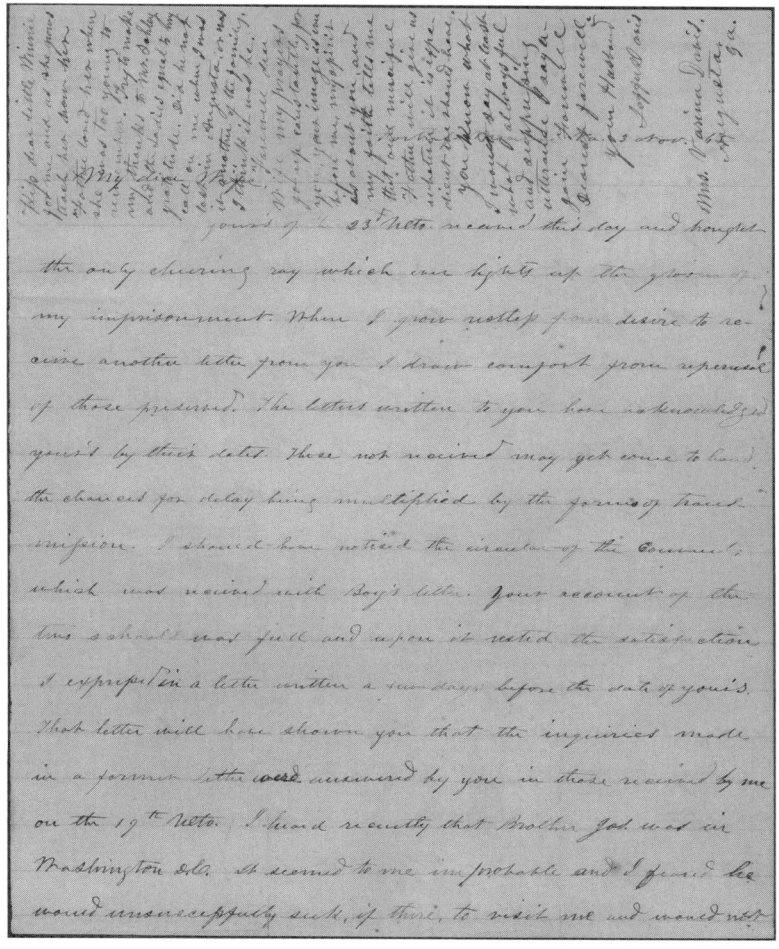

First page of Letter 6 (*November 3-4, 1865*).

Letter 7
(November 21-22, 1856)

F. Monroe 21 Nov. 65

My dear Wife,

I have the happiness to acknowledge your's of the 7th Inst. Had it contained less interesting matter your wish would have been fulfilled. To see your hand is much to me, to learn that your health is improving and our infant well was the best balm which in your absence could be applied to my heart. God be praised for your welfare and for the kind friends He has drawn around you in the day of your affliction. Notwithstanding your assurance that Winnie is so healthy I am anxious because of the want of hair. That combined with a large head suggests to me the necessity for constant exercise in the open air and freedom from causes to excite the brain. I [k]now how watchful and intelligent you are in such matters, but constant observation is not favorable to the perception of a gradual change. I was unwilling to have my hair cut in your absence, and waited with the vain hope of some change which would make it possible for me to see you, until the hair grew so long that it curled, became troublesome and fell out rapidly; it was then trimmed and the shearing product is preserved for you. Your usual wish was thus far followed.

Less than yourself can I claim to be superior to the feeling of resentment for injuries wantonly or maliciously inflicted. I did not mean so much by invoking you to possess your soul in patience[1]: Our heavenly Father merciful to our infirmities cannot require of us superhuman virtues. Our Litany[2] joins together forgiveness of our enemies and the change of their hearts. The voices of nature and religion are from the same divine source, they can only be discordant where one or the other has been perverted. The instinct of self preservation involves resistance to aggression, but it's highest development is freest from vengeance or cruelty. Revelation teaches us to hope for forgiveness if truly repentant; magnanimity compels us to accept the declaration made with such external evidence as is suited to our comprehension; and both combine to exclude from the heart the spirit of persecution, both lead us to forget, rather than to cherish the memories of wrong; so that as soon as the wicked cease from troubling[3] and permit the wounds to heal, the heart fired with grateful love of the Lord, has a mantle of charity broad enough to hide the offenses committed against it.

Your letter of the 13th Inst. has just arrived an advent twice blessed. It brings me pleasing intelligence in regard to the children and relieves you from the dull channel into which my letter was running. It requires all the self control of which I am possessed to think calmly of my separation from you and them. In vain would I summon the conviction that our sufferings are blessings in disguise if my pen were allowed freely to run on the subject of which my heart and mind are most full. You are clearly right in insisting that those at school shall strictly conform to the discipline established. Fortitude and self abnegation so essential to success and happiness are seldom possessed by those who were indulged in childhood. The rigid home discipline of the "dissenters" of Scotland, and of the early "puritans" of New England produced people whose energy overcame all the disadvantages of the soil & climate of both countries, and sent out from each representatives who in every part of the world have been successful in the struggle of life.

The repute of Robert's companion is not good. He probably expected to create a sensation by taking Robt., and may ruin him to your future service. The effect of his European tour will need to be noted if he should offer to renew relations. I have full faith in Maggie's judgment and resolution. If she doubts she will consult you and jointly you will justify my expectations and disprove your own distrust. In a former letter your attention was directed to the possilility [*sic*] of troubles in Canada, and reference made to John and Preston J for information and advice. It would be a severe trial to you to widen the space which separates you from the children and until you can accompany them I pray that there will be no necessity for doing so; and that you may be spared this and all other increase to the crushing burdens that already are impressed upon you.

I wish you would wear a screen over your eye until it is entirely restored, abstaining in the mean time from reading, sewing or other effort by the well eye. The sympathy between the two is such that you should not use either more than is unavoidable. Much as I value your letters I would rather you had not written under such circumstances. The adventurer you mention always was a trifling fellow and was formerly suspected of being unfaithful. His impudence has however passed supposable bounds, & W.W.'s meanness seems to have kept pace with it. They both deserve to be put in the penitentiary for getting money under false pretences. It is intolerable to have one's name used by such sharpers in a manner so humiliating. I hope Maj. W's friends will expose the transaction so that no imitator can repeat the trick. Where is B.P.'s mother and other relatives, and why is she left thus a wanderer? I am sadly disappointed in Joe. his losses should have aroused his energy and kept him at home and at work. Few had a clearer field than he, among his own people.

In the absence of information as to passing events and consequent changes in Missi I can form no definite opinion as to the requirements of the times. The transition state is always perilous and the present one is peculiarily [sic] so. If those who cannot shut their eyes to the evils involved in the social change which has been so suddenly wrought, stand idly by to behold the fulfillment of their forebodings, or vainly attempt to resist a tide which cannot now be arrested, the direction of affairs must fall into incompetent or corrupt hands and accumulating disasters must be the result to make the best of the existing condition is alike required by patriotism and practical sense. The negro is unquestionably to be at last the victim, because when brought into conflict, the inferior race must be overborne; but if it is possible to defer the conflict, & to preserve part of the kind relations heretofore existing between the races, when a life long common interest united them, the object is worthy of an effort. To be successful the policy must be as far removed from the conservatism that rejects every thing new, as from the idealism which would retain nothing which is old. If catch words determine who shall mould the institutions and administer the affairs of the southern states—the deluge. Though neither a spectator nor an actor, a life spent more in the service of my country than in that of my family, leaves me now unable to disengage myself from consideration of public interests; and as you are my only correspondent, you are the unlucky depositary of my speculations, so far as it is permitted to communicate them. [*The last 12 ½ words are at the bottom of the page in his tiny hand, about half the size of his regular one, but perfectly readable.*]

I sincerely regret the sickness of our good friends for those who have been so kind to you are my friends though it should never be in power [*sic*] to show it. You deserve much praise for resisting your desire for the cool air of dewy night, and would equally have deserved it had not your reward been so prompt. And dear little Pie how did she bear the oppressive heat. If Mary[4] knew how little people reflect before speaking of a child, she would care less for their remarks. You recollect how the cat in the cradle was admired. You and the Baby now stand together as in the Photograph. Little Polly's voice pronouncing Father, is still in my ear, unchanged, and so it will remain until I hear her in an altered voice, or cease to hear. But of my feelings it is not my purpose to write, through your own heart they are best expressed.

The best source of patience, is the assurance that the world is governed by infinite wisdom and that He who rules, only permits injustice for some counterbalancing good of which the sufferer cannot judge. The decrees of Providence are wrought by human agencies, but how often had it happened that resistance was the manner in which the agent was appointed to work. If then we have conscientiously resolved and assiduously labored, should we not accept the result as a step towards better things, though to our blindness it may seem fatal to the better cause. Did the Lord always grant our purest prayers when and as they are offered, what misery and remorse should we not entail upon ourselves. Daily and nightly I beseech the Father to conduct you and our little ones to the place where you should be, trusting that He will protect and guide you all, and if it be His will, reunite me with you wherever it is best that you & I be.

[*This ends a page of the manuscript beginning with "I sincerely regret." The whole page is in JD's minuscule handwriting.*]

I am very sorry that the newspapers have distressed you by accounts of my condition and treatment, not seeing them, had hoped that recently the object had been to represent both as better than they were, and preferred that you should have the comfort thus to be derived. When by your letter of Oc. 23^{d}. I saw the the [*sic*] reverse was the fact, I yielded to your renewed request and wrote a minute description of my room, its furniture, the beats of the sentinels etc. etc. etc. that part of my letter was objected to and was rewritten accordingly. Let me renew the caution against believing the statements of correspondents in regard to me. To calumniate a state prisoner and thus either gratify or excite hatred against him is an old device, and never was a fairer opportunity presented to do so without the fear of contradiction, than is offered in my case. My health is better than it was months ago, my food is suited to my health and as abundant as I desire. You had better abandon your purpose to send me delicacies, and remember that care for food or for raiment was never one of my sins.[5] My sleep is less disturbed than formerly, and except for the local disease heretofore described, and which changes the place but keeps the pain, I have no physical ailment to mention. Notice was given to me some days since of the arrival of a trunk with clothes for me, a list of which was handed to me, I infer they were sent by you. The trunk was sent to Dr. Craven who is temporarily absent, expected to return to-day I have been informed. Mr. Clay I am told is unwell to-day, I wish it was in power [*sic*] to be with him, as he is represented at such times to become sadly dejected. His wife has probably gone to Washington with hopes natural for her to entertain. God grant their realization.

Nov. 22[d]. It is six months since we parted and I know no more of the purpose in regard to me than I did then. Measured by painful anxiety for you and your helpless charge those months are to me many, many years. From the anguish and double painful trial because I could learn nothing of you, I have extracted the consolation of increased pride and fully sustained confidence, in her who is to me the dearest object in life, in pain and sickness the hand that soothed and relieved was wanting, but the spirit always answered to a summons and when natural vision was suppressed would stand before me in the light of memory. I do take care of my health, all the motives you enumerate are ever before me, and others of which you are less apt to think, furnish the strongest inducement to desire life and strength to vindicate my conduct; at least to posterity and for my family. Be hopeful, trust in the "faithful Promiser".[6] When you write to B H or his pretty daughter, or to Bson[7] please mention me in most friendly terms. Give my best love to Ma and Margaret. Kiss little V. for me, tell Maggie and the boys how much I love them and how constantly I pray for them.

I could have anticipated the effect on Chesnut[8], of whom I have always been very fond. When you write to his wife give my love to them, etc. etc. My paper is nearly exhausted and warns me to say Farewell. My dear Wife how I long once more to speak or even to write to you without restraint. But let us not repine for what we have not. Rather rejoicing in what we have, let us with faith and charity look out for a better 'morrow. May the Lord have you in his holy keeping and send the Comforter to your sorrowing heart. Shut out from the ever changing world I live in the past, with a vividness only thus to be accounted for all the events of all the years of our love rise before me and bear witness how very dear you are to your Husband.

Mrs. Varina Davis-Augusta, Ga.   Jeffn Davis

[*The last quarter of this page is in JD's minuscule hand.*]

I have nothing yet in regard to the course to be taken in my case. The news papers have recently represented that I am to be tried to test the doctrine on which I acted, & against it establish the authority of the general government. The question involved has been the basis of political divisions in the United States since the second year of the administration of the elder Adams, it was earnestly and fully discussed in the colonial times, and reached back through European history to the reign of King Solomon's son. Many men have died for it, but their condemnation was not accepted as a decision concluding the question. —— Since my last letter, a friend has sent to me "Schönberg Cotta family"; my eyes cause me to read at intervals, otherwise I found it so interesting that it would have tempted me to read through it without intermission. My mark is at Eva's story, p. 370. and my paper does not permit any remarks on the book as far as read. For relief to the eyes I frequently change the type. Have now Humboldt's Cosmos, Irving's Washington and Allison's Marlborough from the post library. My Bible, Prayer Book and a Dictionary of the Bible are my endless resource.

Give my love in terms you will know how to employ to my dear little Polly, to Jefferson and William. Kiss little Winnie for one who loves her and prays that she may yet know him. Also to Ma. and Maggie, who I hope are comfortably protected against the rigorous winter. I am better than when I lately wrote to you. The drier & purer air of my room has caused much improvement in my health since leaving the casemate; and since Dr. Craven has furnished me with food nothing which is necessary has been wanting. You cannot be content, yet you may be assured that I am as well as circumstances permit. Let not imaginary evils distress you, let us strive for the patience which can say sincerely, Father not my will, but thine be done. Farewell my dearest, soon I hope the truth will disperse error, and calumny & restore me to you, to be happier as made better by the chastening correction of the merciful, loving Father. Your Husband Jefferson Davis

Mrs. Varina Davis - Augusta Ga.

Last page of Letter 7 (*November 26, 1865*).

Letter 8
(Novermber 26-27, 1865)

Sunday 26 Nov. 1865

My dear wife,

Many thanks to you for your letter of the 16th Inst. And its enclosure, the letter of my beloved daughter. Sweet is it to witness her filial tenderness, but very sad to see such evidence of her anxiety for me. I hope you have written to her encouragingly, and that she will look forward to my coming as an event which will bring her relief. To-day as I read the service it was ever in my mind that the same words were prompting the same thoughts to you as to me. You I hope had the benefit of association with church members, and that union of prayer the value of which can only be realized by those who have been deprived of it. Though God is omnipresent, and his love enables us to look up to him with trust; though we are taught that the lonely sinner is sought after by the good shepherd, and that he will rejoice in bringing him back to the fold; the heart even in its least expressible feeling profits by communion with those who sympathize.

Little Polly seems to think she has charge of her Brothers and to feel the solicitude of mature years. She will I am sure be all you expect if allowed to mature as designed by her nature. Few very few are equal to that seemingly simple course of education. In a public school the rules must generally be framed to suit the hardest characters, and the course graduated to suit classes, instead of corresponding to the special adaptions of scholars. I have in regard to boys thought there were compensating advantages. If the schooling had been designed for packing and moving through crowded lanes, the Button-makers would have been more wise than Shenstone.[1] And so boys who are to engage closely in the conflicts of life, had better be pruned down to its patterns.

Nov. 27. The day blessed by our Saviour has passed, the busy world has again gone to its weekly mail, and may the Lord whose precious blood was shed to atone for the sins of man inspire all to labor for each other's good. To me days differ mainly by the memories you generally mingle. Your care protected me from many ills, your hand assuaged suffering, your voice told of happy things and breathed the music sweetest to my ears, your pious spirit recalled me from thorny paths and led me into the bosom of the Church. "Woe is me that I am constrained to dwell with Meshech".[2]

Mr. Clay has been suffering lately with like affliction to that which has troubled me. His Wife is in Washington, I hope she may not suffer if disappointed, more than is due to the cause she advocates, but the light in which she views it, is too different from that in which it appears to the authorities to qualify her for the office of a solicitor.

I regret that Mary Jane did not see my little friend at the Moravian school. Her claim to attention could not have been understood. Fannie's husband is to me a source of deep solicitude. "Pleasures are like poppies spread"[3] The disjointed news I see in the papers indicate confusion if not conflict in the civil government of Missi; but of its nature I cannot judge. It is unfortunate that any job should be given to a machine so untried. Hereabout as elsewhere, it is said, the negroes have expectations which may be mischievous, when the close of the year the time of their anticipated fulfillment arrives. Their characteristic improvidence will bring enough of discontent to justify caution even had no delusive hopes been nurtured; and I would impress upon you the exercise of all your judgment in the selection of the safest place within the limits of your bounds. You have friends near you who are so much better informed than myself that it would be worse than useless for me to express an opinion. The Lord preserve you from all evil.

The dressing gown you sent, the night shirts and other things are great comfort to me. The m[ar]k on the handkerchiefs no fingers save your's could make, and this leads me to fear you have been wearing yourself down by sewing on the other articles also. I would not have it so, though doubly dear to me is any thing you have touched for your health is to my comfort most needful of all things within your control.

I have nothing yet in regard to the course to be taken in my case. The news papers have recently represented that I am to be tried to test the doctrine on which I acted, & against it establish the authority of the general government. The

question involved has been the basis of political
divisions in the United States since the second
year of the Administrations of the elder Adams,
it was earnestly and finally discussed in the colonial times and reaches back through European
history to the reign of King Solomon's son. Many
men have died for it, but their condemnation was
not accepted as a decision concluding the question. —since my last letter, a friend has sent to me
"Schonburg Cotta family" my eyes cause me to
read at intervals, otherwise I found it so interesting
that it would have tempted [me] to read through it
without intermission. My mark is at Eva's story,
p. 370 and my paper does not permit any remarks
on the book as far as read. For relief to the eyes I
frequently change the type. Have now Humboldt's
Cosmos, Irving's Washington and Allison's Marlborough from the post library. My Bible—Prayer
Book and a dictionary of the Bible are my endless
resource.

Give my love in terms you will know how
to employ to my dear little Polly & to Jefferson
and William. Kiss little Winnie for one who loves
her and prays that she may yet know him. Also
to Ma. and Maggie, who I hope are comfortably
protected against the vigorous winter. I am better than when I lately wrote to you. The drier and
purer air of my room has caused much improvement in my health since leaving the casemate,
and since Dr. Craven has furnished me with food
nothing which is necessary has been wanting. you
cannot be content, yet you may be assured that I
am as well as circumstances permit. Let not imaginary evils distress you, let us strive for the patience
which can say sincerely, Father not my will, but
thine be done. Farewell my dearest, soon I hope

the truth will disperse error and calumny & restore me to you, to be made happier as made better by the chastening correction of the merciful, loving Father. Your Husband.

Mrs. Varina Davis–Augusta Ga.   Jeffn Davis

Letter 9
(December 2-3, 1865)

Fortress Monroe, Va. 2^d Dec. 65

My dear Wife,

I have the pleasure to acknowledge your's of the 21st Ulto. with four letters enclosed. The information in regard to the children is very consolotary [? *"t" not crossed*]. The exactness and directness of my dear little daughter is truly gratifying. The reflection manifested in her answer to your inquiries shows progress in the development of her mind and a sense of responsibility beyond her years. I feel both pride and hope increasing with her growth. God grant that it may be permitted to me to give a Father's hand to her as she moves on in the trials of life; but if I may not lead her, the Protector of the Orphan will not, I pray and trust allow her to want an earthly Father's care. It was very kind of the Bishop to show her such marked attention. Similar kindness though in a less pronounced manner, was shown to me under like circumstances and have always been gratefully remembered, even from my ninth year when the favors were first received. Was

the affection of the chest of which your Ma. writes
produced by the climate? She did not suffer thus in
former years did she? At her age[1] such attacks are
not to be disregarded as once they might have been.

No more than yourself do I grieve that our
boys must grow up with the sense of self dependence. To have enough to prepare them for the
struggle of life by a full education, would be better
than poverty; but the worst is such impressions as
Billy's reminiscence proclaims. Of all the injuries,
the unmanly, wanton outrages upon my helpless
Wife and children are the hardest for me to forgive;
I sought to keep their hearts free for the pure pulsa-
tions of universal christian love. Bad, bad was the
hand that came to scatter tares upon that virgin
field where yet had grown no evil weeds.[2] Should
your pious prayers be heard, in that home life for
which you hope, we will endeavor to cultivate our
crops so at last to separate the bad without serious
diminution of the good. The way and the time will
bring us to the appointed end, and then if we can
look back upon proper and consistent efforts on our
part, we can bow in calm submission to the decree,
however unlike it may be to the result we sought to
achieve.

My days drag heavily on, to what I have no
means to direct or to foresee. Having no communication with the outer world, except with you, and
in that restricted by the judgement of the Comdg[3]
officer as to what should be sent, those who choose
to falsify my conduct have as safe a task as slanderer
could desire. So freely has advantage been taken of
the opportunity even in regard to matters of public
record and public notoriety, that you should have
known how little you could trust the statements in
regard to occurrences in my prison. It is true that

nothing happens which does not somehow pass to
newspaper correspondents, but as is usually the case
with monopolies, they abuse their privilege by per-
verting their knowledge and building a superstruc-
ture with but little regard to the foundation. You say
the papers tell you every thing, but I warn you that
the things they tell you are not realities. The example you give will illustrate, The "new" overcoat I
have not received; though probably when the statement was published on which you relied as telling
at least one fact, it had reached this post. The matter being of such public importance as to have been
followed in its progress though the tailor's shop, and
down the Bay[4], the journals may give you the future
history before it is known to me. In a late letter I
notified you of the arrival of the trunk you sent to
me, and I have enough of warm clothes. When you
were told that your inquiries were "noted", it was
to prevent you from supposing they were neglected,
and you were expected to draw the conclusion that
I had been prevented from answering them as they
were asked. It would be very agreeable to me to give
you such description of my room and its surround-
ing as would enable you entirely to comprehend the
physical objects with which I am connected. The
newspapers here announced the change made in
the garrison by the publication of the orders in the
case to which I may refer you.

My daily walks continue, the hour dependent
upon Genl. Miles['] engagements, as I only go
out when he can be present. Dr. Craven visits me
when needful, and his good wife sees that meals
and clean clothes are duly sent to me. Do not
make to yourself causeless anxiety, but the rather
patiently wait for the fulfillment, believing that
an unseen hand is directing our fortune accord-

ing to the omniscience and infinite mercy which guides and governs all things. He gives us a hope that man cannot destroy, a refuge that man cannot invade; the foretaste of which is the trusting communion of loving hearts, whose correspondence superior to the electric, is neither limited by the wasting power of space, nor stopped by interposing oceans. Thus can I say to you, "Far off thou art, but ever nigh;" etc. etc. etc..[5]

Sunday morning. 3. Dec. 65—The bright sun and mild temperature welcomes the blessed day of rest, which calls the redeemed to meet together, and rejoice that their Saviour [*last word written very large and heavy over another word*] has risen again, and sitteth in the place prepared for the faithful.

Deprived of the opportunity to assemble with the members of the church there is left to me the spirit communion with those I daily and nightly summon to meet together in His name who is ever present, and thus I have read the morning service, including the lessons both of the Dominical and Calendar day. How full they are of Providences —— Holy innocence closes the mouths of fiercest beasts and triumphs over the crafts and subtleties of wicked men; conscious sinfulness silences those who came to arraign a guilty mortal, and entrap the Righteous judge; repentance working deliverance to an oppressed and dispersed people; the prayers of the church effecting the miraculous preservation of one apostle from the fate which had a short time before fallen upon another.

I was much pleased with the book you recommended, but could but feel that the object with which it was written created severity it seemed to me injustice towards the Priests and Nuns[.] If they had been so bad, their training could hardly have produced the high characters presented, the heroes and heroines of the reformation. Those I knew from close association appeared to me very good. Have you read the "Gayworthys"?[6] An officer on duty for the day with the guard set over me, handed the book to me with a request that I would give him my opinion of it. It is a work of great power. Like the Schönberg the characters are only what in pharmacy is called a carrier, and like it also the purpose is in familiar form, to present religious opinions.

It is evidently by a woman, she must have lived in a rural district of New England, and I would think have travelled out of it so as to realize its peculiarities. Some of the expressions and scenes suggested to me that it might have been written by a bright girl, whose account of the "learned women" of her neighborhood so much amused you. Drifting from Puritanism towards Universalism, and hanging about Election, the conclusion is not so well defined as Luther's was. It is well worth reading attentively.

Allison's Marlborough is graphic and interesting. One who compares it with McCauley's account of the same person, would be led to concur with Sir H. Walpole's opinion in regard to history.[7] I find Irving's Washington better even than I used to think, his success is such as your acquaintance of a former time, described that of her Father to be, in treating of the same subject.

I saw Mr. Clay yesterday, as we passed I inquired of his health, he replied that he was improving. To me he looked badly. His Wife, lately was reported to be in Washington and may still be there. No doubt if she fails in her main purpose, she will seek to visit her Husband. I referred in my remark about misapprehension of events, to the opinion J.E.D.[8] had given in regard to a Commander for the Army in Georgia, but il n'importe[9], time is said to put all things even, and may do so in that case when circumstances are more favorable to exposition of truth[.]

Many thanks to you for your attention in writing so frequently, hereafter I would suggest that you might limit your labors to those who are the best correspondents and let them distribute. I could not write daily as you wish because I am not allowed to keep stationery. When it is specially granted, it has to be accounted for, the whole being returned written or blank as may be. There is such sameness in my life that you have little cause to regret my letters not being more frequent, with you it is otherwise and the Atty. Genl. will probably indulge us by forwarding your letters as often as you write. His past courtesy warrants such expectation. Dr. Craven was not connected with the former garrison being a medical purveyor, his is now Post Surgeon and I hope will not be relieved. That however will probably depend upon the necessity for continuing volunteer Surgeons in the service. I have a high opinion of his professional skill and if another were his equal in general knowledge he must want for a time the special knowledge of my case which Dr. Craven possesses. The Chaplain of the Pa. Regt left with it, there was also a Post Chaplain who has been here about thirty years, I am told, his name is Cheevers, the one for whom I expect you inquired is named Kerfoot, he has been mustered out with the Vol. Regt. To which he was attached. Genl. Miles still commands the district of which this Post is the Head Quarters.

What was the matter with little Winnie? Please have her kept as much as possible in the open air, and as little as possible in the way of excitement. You will understand me. I wish you would always write fully about her. To hear of what she does keeps me acquainted with her as she changes. Send the full measure of a Father's love to little Polly, to the big and the little boy. Though the measure you sent me is suggestive of a speedy misapplication of the diminutive to the latter. I am more free from physical ill now than for some time past. Have no information bearing on any action in my case, and it would be useless to speculate. William B. Reed of Philad[10] recently tendered to me his professional services in a very kind and handsome letter. Thos. J. Wharton, C.E. Hooker and Fulton Anderson are the Missi Lawyers who offered their services and were recognized as counsel by the U.S. Secty. of State.[11] I requested permission to acknowledge his kindness by a letter, it was not granted.

Farewell, my beloved Wife may the greatest good be conferred upon you; the peace which lifts above the troubles of this world and opens the view of the world to come attend you; and may our merciful Father restore us to each other that we may gather our children around us and calmly prepare for the final summons, aiding and sustaining each other in the works both for time and eternity until that last [*here the writing of the manuscript stops at the end of page 8 and resumes, crosswise, at the top of page 1:*] call shall be given. Though formally taking leave of you you will not be left. In the stillness of your quiet hour a Husband's love is around you, and to the most High his imperfect, unworthy prayer ascends that the all seeing eye may keep watch over his sorrowing Wife and helpless child.

Ever affectionately
          Your Husband
          Jeffn. Davis
Mrs. Varina Davis
          Augusta,
          Ga..

Letter 9 (*December 02, 1865*). Top: p. 4 and 1. Bottom: p. 2 and 3.

Letter 10
(December 7-8, 1865)

Fortress Monroe Va. 7th Dec. 65

Mrs. Varina Davis,
My beloved Wife,

I thank you for your ever welcome letter of
the 27th Ulto. enclosing a letter from Jefferson and
one from his teacher. The account given of him
is to me the most gratifying which was possible.
I am truly grateful that he has fallen into hands
where the method and object of discipline so well
accords with our own views. The lessons in Arith-
metic etc. etc. though important are less valuable
than those which it is less ostensibly the purpose to
teach. These latter ones make impressions never to
be wholly effaced, and determine whether the boy
will grow to be a man who deserves success and
by his character commands respect where he is
most intimately known. His reference to the Hymn
is a touching evidence of the gentle affection so
early manifested by him. It was a hopeful sign
that he was always a favorite with our servants. I
trust he will be a comforting stay to your declin-

ing years and a reliable protection to the other children in future time. I am deeply impressed by the kindness of the Bishop[1], and that of the priests who have so nobly shown their readiness to do their Master's work in relieving the afflicted, and protecting the fatherless. They have sent thus, the sweetest solace to one, in the condition of him who went down from Jerusalem to Jericho.[2] Yes, I feel with you, that God has been very good to us.

Reagan I knew to be a true hearted, consistent man and I never gave the least heed to the newspaper reports which attributed to him participation in censorious remarks against me, during his confinement at Fort Warren.[3] Some men I had to trust because of the confidence others had in them. When disaster fell upon me their desertion did not surprise me. It grieves me to learn that Seddon and Mallory[4] are still in confinement. Some time since I was told that all the persons in their condition had been released, and recently saw that Davis had been arrested, also that a general petition for his release had been gotten up in N.C. which it was expected would be effectual.[5] The proverb in relation to the desire of misery for companionship is not realized by me in this matter of imprisonment. I would that like one of old it were for me to say—I alone am left.[6] To me, as it must to you, it is sometimes a puzzle to find the rule of discrimination. Mr. Clay is for the second time suffering from a boil. He has not heard, I understand, from his wife[7] since her arrival at Washington. As he has not been out to walk for several days I have not seen him. To one bowed down by an overwhelming trouble it is unfortunate to have hopes excited which cannot be fulfilled. In such a situation Hume's[8] balance is peculiarily [sic] to be sought. As natural rights belong only to those who can maintain them, so natural affections and excitements are only safe to those who are not unnaturally restrained.

I have been reading "thoughts on personal religion" by Dr. Goulburn.[9] His instructions as to Prayer have impressed me particularly. How like is the experience of men. It is no small encouragement to a sinner striving for a better state, to find those who have at least in the world's estimation, won the crown of glory, had passed through such tribulation as he is beset with. Did it never occur to you how much evil is done by the use of a text startling in its terms and so iterated and reiterated that any explanation of it's meaning by reference to other texts bearing on the same subject is lost. It occurred to me after last writing to you that something of that kind might have happened to you in regard to forgiveness; and I regretted not having pointed out the illustration of his meaning which our Saviour gave in the parable of the King who took an account of his servants.[10] When we shall pass into the future state of pure intelligence so as to judge not by external signs but by the inner motives how different men will appear to each other from the estimates of their carnal life. May it not be that we shall then find our most earnest efforts at self examination brought us but to a poor knowledge of ourselves.

Though my prison life does not give me the quiet of solitude its isolation as to intercourse affords abundant opportunity for turning the thoughts inward; and if my self love, not to say sense of justice, would have resisted the reckless abuse of my enemies; I am humbled by your unmerited praise, it teaches me what I ought to be, and lifts my eyes to Him whose all sufficient grace alone can raise me to your ideal standard. Were we together, your aid would bless my efforts, without you, without the communion of the Church, but not alone, nor without remembrance that the burthen is not permitted to exceed the strength, I live and hope.[11]

The "heavy erasures" concerning which you inquire, assuming that they were made by me, as the Atty. Genl. had politely informed you that he did not do it, were not by my choice. To your repeated requests to be informed as to my room, my clothes, and the change of garrison as affecting me, I replied in the letter to which you refer. Two leaves containing the answers to the two first questions were returned to me as matter which would not be forwarded, and they were rewritten omitting the answer described. Subsequently my attention was called to a sentence on another page responding to your inquiry about the new garrison and stating a consequent alteration in the matter of sentinels, which I was required to obliterate. I drew the pen through it and sent it back. Genl. Miles afterwards told me that it had still been legible as I left it, and added something not distinctly heard, beyond the point of main interest that the letters had been sent. I can readily understand by my own wishes in regard to you, the desire you felt for the minute knowledge of the little things about me which those answers contained; but as they would only enable you more fully to perceive those points on which it is least pleasant to dwell, you may easily adopt in this case the practice of the optimist.

A staff officer at these Hd. Qrs.[12] informed me that the ornamental hair work which was sent to you by a young Lady, had been found in the possession of a colored woman of this neighborhood, and in reply to inquiry I asked him to send it to Mr. Lyons at Richmond.[13] You can give further directions there.

I am very much obliged to Mr. Huntington, but unless he has some reason to expect success he had better not forward his purchase.[14] Experentia docet, sed indocti in hoc non discant.[15] Those who have made even a small crop of cotton will have a return exceeding what a full crop would have brought in former years. The only questions which I have seen discussed in regard to the cotton production of future years seem to me very microscopic. But I am constantly reminded of my exclusion from information by the seeming incongruity of the most public transactions.

My incarceration followed four years of terrible war. The North put forth its whole capacity on land and sea, by ball and bayonet striving to retain the South in one government with it; the South strained every nerve to maintain a separate existence: by the newspaper to day I see that the North as represented in Congress stands quite united to keep the South out of the Legislative halls of the Union, and the South wistfully looking at the closed entrance stands outside, & there she is told she has all the time been inside.

In regard to the action to be taken in my case I have like the weary knife grinder no story to tell.[16] The few papers I see are no doubt seen by you and the indications are not favorable to any speedy result. Mr. Guthrie[17] is in the Senate with Garrett Davis representing Kentucky. Reverdy Johnson is also there. Mr. Buchannan's [sic] book is I understand on sale, and I hope soon to see it.[18] The news papers have given it unkind criticism; critics however are not believed to read the books they "review".

Some time since I wrote to you calling your attention to the reports about movements among the negroes, which if exagerated [*sic*] were not to be overlooked as the pressure of winter on such an improvident people would increase a small spark into a fire. In some of the towns within your bounds there will probably be found such military organization as will there give greater security than in the country. Of this however your own judgement aided by the counsel of some of our well informed friends, will decide much better than I can. It is possible not to complain, it is not possible to avoid feeling such needless deprivation. But so many singular incidents combined to produce the present situation that it seems wrong to oppose it as the work of human will, and in vain regret to run backwards over the course of time to contemplate what might have been but cannot be. The ways of Him who doeth all things well are inscrutable to man. Let us learn to say not mine but thy will be done.[19] The bitterness which caused me to be so persistently slandered, has created a sentiment which will probably find vent in congressional speeches, and test all your christian fortitude. Remember that the end is not yet. A fair inquiry will show how "false witnesses have risen up against me and laid to my charge things that I knew not of.[20] If you will recall the very early period when I was warned by letter that an emissary had been sent to Montgomery[21] to assassinate me, you will see misconception of my position and a cruel desire for my destruction are not new born. When the truth is revealed the more honorable and manly of my enemies will recoil from further association with the others. Truth and the common sense of justice will generally protect the innocent, where the trial is according to the due course of law, and is sure to vindicate the memory of a victim.

Kiss dear little Winnie for me, give my tenderest love to Maggie and Jeff and Billy when you write, also to dear Margaret and Ma. There is in all my trials one from which I shrink and you will not need an explanation of my inability to express my feelings towards you and the children as was my habit in former days. There is an unseen hand which upholds me save when any thoughts are concentrated on those objects of my dearest love and greatest solicitude. Perhaps He will give me that strength hereafter. In the many friends He has raised up for you there is the promise of that peace to come. I fear that you have confined yourself too much to the house. Your mental anxiety and physical ills will act and react on each other. If you can master one it will help you to overcome the other. You will try for my sake, and that of our young children who have now the directing care of one parent only. Have you heard from John or Preston[22] in regard to the apprehended convulsions in that quarter. There should be a preconcerted plan in the event of removal becoming necessary. The good Bishop might then be of inestimable service. As I have heretofore written to you, the want of definite information renders me unable to form an opinion and you will not understand me as venturing a conclusion.

Please give my thanks and kindest regard to Mr. Schley and family. Grateful for the kindness to Miss P.C. I will not be envious of what would be to me a happiness, perhaps their goodness makes it to them a pleasure. My fire has gone out and as I have no present means of rekindling it, will bid you good night. May angels keep watch over you—I pray, pray, pray—— —

Nov. 8 [*really, Dec.*]—Another day has succeeded the night. The Sun has risen bright and the cold bracing air invites animal life to activity. To me there is the same monotonous round of a prisoner's life, in military confinement such as is not known to the usages of War in cases like mine. I am however thankful for the power to bear, and trustful that the power will still be given to me to bear in patience.

In a former letter I mentioned to you that the trunk you had sent with clothes had arrived. I notice that the shirts are new, and it excites the inquiry whether you have been robbed of those which you took with your baggage when you left me in Richmond.[23] The new overcoat which you spoke of in a former letter has been delivered to me. Do you know anything of Burton and Frank.[24] I never was at Athens, but have heard of it as a pleasant place.[25] If the field where the events of Jordans [*sic*] critique occurred was near to Drury's bluff, Col. Melton knows how my designs were frustrated and how little the promise accorded with the action on the unwise plan substituted for mine. A letter to Mr. Seddon put it beyond the power of any one to falsify that affair, it was sent by Genl. B[26] the day before he undertook the execution [*of*] his own plan, to account for the change he made, and from which when it failed he endeavored to escape by blaming Whiting and Ransom [*last two words smaller and fainter than preceding two*].

Have you any knowledge of Northrop's whereabouts and condition.[27] I told Holmes what must if N. heard it have shown him that he was not set adrift; and I wished him not to be mistaken, as to my acts. If I was not mistaken in his character he would not willingly do any one injustice.

Farewell my dear Wife, if as appears to be indicated I am turned over to the civil authorities, the chance to see you, and to prepare for my defence by intercourse with counsel, will probably be better than now. May God bless me again with the sight of you, and may he guide and protect you until he receives you into the mansion prepared for the blessed followers of the Son. Ever affectionately your Husband

Jeffn. Davis

[*The hand writing on this page gets smaller and smaller until the "Jeffn. Davis" on the bottom edge has no letter taller than an eighth of an inch and the dots under the tail of the "n" are infinitesimal, but they are there.*]

Letter 11
(December 30, 1865-January 1, 1866)

Fortress Monroe 30 Dec 1865

My dear Wife,

Yours of the 14 Inst. enclosing that of our little Daughter, reached me yesterday. The "pictures" which you notice as having been omitted were not probably line and shade, but word paintings and found in the text. The preferences you express for mythical symbols over your own idealities marks a happy state of realization which I cannot command. Indeed one of the difficulties usually met when I attempt to express an opinion on a metaphysical subject, is the inappropriateness of language drawn from material objects to describe spiritual things; so much the more is this the case in regard to pictorial representations. The artist in his working nature mingles with my contemplation of his study. Living souls devoutly offering praise to God present spirituality supreme over matter, and it is perhaps therefore that the simple singing of an excited congregation of "Methodists", has stirred in my heart a deeper devotional

feeling than the noble ceremonial of the High
Mass, with all the brilliant surroundings which in
the richly endowed Cathedrals are associated with
it. All modes of christian worship are in themselves good, they are the different kind of roads
suited to the great variety of travellers, and why
not to the different moods of the same traveller, if
by such diversion he may the more certainly reach
the end of his journey. I do not mean such separation as would lose the right of communion with
the church chosen as the one preferred. In most
situations we realize the evils of our own condition and see the benefits of another. The change
if it be made, may reverse the forms by reversing
the light, and bring regrets which would have been
avoided by a [*freer?*] observation and closer inquiry.
Luther was a benefactor of mankind with whom
few will bear a comparison. But while his protest
against the sale of indulgences is most gratefully
remembered, there is much in his subsequent
career to be covered with the mantle of charity,
and which he must have acknowledged he did not
forsee [*sic*]. My early impressions and continuing
affection for the Priests of "Saint Thomas"[1] led me
to clothe all their brethren in a moral robe as white
as the toga of my early friends . In Havanna[2] [*sic*]
I first learned how great was the mistake & elsewhere and subsequently was forced to believe that
the vows which had seemed so well to fit the Roman Priest for the ministry of God, were in some
places and with some, perhaps in all places,—
"cheap as custom-house oaths." So without aban-
doning mon premier amour[3], I rest my hopes with
more satisfaction and security on another organization. The catholicity of St. Paul suits me well.
According to Northrop none but the Papists can

be saved, according to Mx[4] all the Papists must be condemned; so between these sectarians both honest and talented, the Lamb of God was sacrificed in vain. How much better to hope that, though the flocks be scattered on a thousand hills they are all cared for by the great Shepherd, who will seek every sheep that is lost without inquiring from which flock it is astray.[5]

When the Lord shall open the many mansions of His Father's house to receive his own, I would that we should be there together, but more oh! most [*written over "almost," erased*] I would, that we should all be there. Thus to mingle earthly with devotional love would once have seemed to me forbidden; but recent reflection has modified that view; so that the New Testament appears to me as a light leading the natural affections to the hallowed and exalted condition in which they become vessels of honor bearing incense acceptable to the Creator. Our Saviour in the agony of the cross remembered the temporal need of his Mother. The Apostle whom He loved sums up the duties of the Christian in the sentence, Love one another[6].

If we are permitted in our old age to be the more closely united by the flight of the herd which once crowded so densely around us, I shall find in the change more than an equivalent, counting it as Paddy would say "the goin of a loss"[7]. For that quondam friend of your's whose defection has evidently pained you, I must offer a defense. You will no doubt be surprised that I should be her apologist. You may not remember that her Husband blamed her because his resignation was offered, that he was striving to regain the lost ground, that she had been reared to regard employment under the government as the only worthy and

safe means of livelihood; and independence or
fidelity to the professional courtier is the impossible offence. She would regard it as unreasonable,
incredible that any thing different from her course
should have been expected. The things to which I
objected were conclusive of the want of sensibility, of pride, and of morality, compared to which
this seems to me a peccadillo. So if the first were
pardonable the last not more clearly proud, should
be overlooked, as conduct which was in character,
which was not intended to be offensive, and which
has enabled you to make a discovery. You were
probably remembered with as much affection as
selfishness permits, and with such regard as generosity and sincerity receives from those who have
neither. As to her Land what could you expect
after the revelations made to you in the matter of
contributions etc, - etc,? We are not in the trials of
Indus; though our adversity may like a furnace be
proving our friends. If it be ordained that we shall
be restored to each other, we shall be better able to
forgive those who have been false, than they will
be to enjoy the proceeds of their treachery. The
lessons of these times will better fit us to teach our
children, and may we not hope better prepare us
for that valley which lies beyond the hill of life.

Mrs. Clay has been here for several days—visiting her Husband in his prison. She left this evening, sent me word that she expected to return and
would endeavor in Washington to get permission
to see me during her next visit. I have no information as to her prospect in regard to the release of
her Husband, and will not do more than express
the hope that her efforts will succeed.

Without good reason I am very anxious
about Jeff. He was expected to spend the holidays

in Montreal. I cannot telegraph or I would inquire in that mode. You will no doubt hear from them at Christmas, and will probably have written to me before this reaches you. Oh! Lord let thy mercy be upon us, In Thee have I trusted.[8]

Dec. 31. This is the last day of a year eventful and to us sorrowful, what the morrow may bring forth or of what it may be the beginning it is to me especially not given to foresee, but I seek to be comforted by the faith that all things are set in order by infinite wisdom and goodness. Your perplexities and distress grieve me sorely. Stripped of property your task would be difficult enough if no obstructions were thrown in your way, but being like myself a prisoner, though less rigorously confined, and by the necessity of the case separated from our children; it is too hard that you should to this mountain of trouble have superadded those weights at which you hint with sufficient distinctness.

I entirely concur with you as to Maggie but hope there may be no cause to require her return to you. The danger would probably be less now than when you were in Savannah, yet there are many objections to such a course and many inducements for keeping her steadily at the School. My own experience does not lead me to expect that proselytism will be attempted on a child of Protestant parents; nor at her tender age is it likely that other than good impressions will be retained.

Those doctrinal points which have been so fruitful of casuistry, could not be understood and therefore would not be long remembered by so young a child. Her gentle and loving nature requires the patient, forgiving treatment which is not to be found as fully in more secular schools.

The favorable impression she seems to have made, by her account of the petting she receives, is an advantage of which she should not be lightly deprived, nor should it's growth be checked by needless interposition.

I saw the account of "Jeddy's"[9] arrest but could not anticipate any serious consequence. He was probably supposed to have been an officer of the Alabama[10] and if he had his parole would in that case be released upon showing it, but if he had no papers with him, his statement of his true position and past service could be easily verified, that I cannot doubt he is at large. His Brother either should not have taken him away or should have kept him there. I suspect he was sent back to take charge of Minnie, it was hardly thought that he should return to his Mother.[11] We did not pursue the proper course (I fear) when he was a school-boy under our care.[12] Discipline in childhood, can rarely be dispensed with, except at the cost of learning later in life and under harder teachers the lessons which should have been early taught.

Do not understand me as having become a convert to the use of harsh means. Uniformity and gentleness I still think to be better than severity. In the government of beasts or of men, I believe harshness is requisite in direct proportion to the incompetence of the ruler. Such at least has been my observation of overseers, Horse-breakers.— School-masters, Parents & public-officers.—

It is no [not?] difficult on account of the different tempers of children to manage several together; so as to require obedience of both without suggesting the idea of partiality. You have a fair chance with little Winnie, and I am prepared for

all you say, and more than you say, of her brightness and goodness. Your narratives are incorporated with her likeness and thus she grows in my
mind as she does in your eyes. Tell her how glad
I was that she took your pencil to send me a message and a kiss—the latter I have taken off.

I feared the affect of so cold a climate on
Ma. With coming age the change should be to a
warmer rather than a colder climate. It is natural also that she should wish to return to her old
home, now that the cause for her departure for it
is removed. Should she do so, what is proposed in
regard to Margaret and Billy? Would the former
like for a time to stay at the Sault au Recollect,
and take lessons in such branches as would give
her useful and pleasant employment? Is the latter
equal to a place with his Brothers at Lennoxville?
Again I say your trials grieve me sorely. Seldom
has a Wife and a Mother been more sadly tried,
and I can do nothing to relieve or sustain you. Let
not your solicitude for me interfere with any practicable arrangement which may be presented by
possible change of circumstance. We are powerless
to aid each other and must bow to the fate which
tears us apart. My spirit dear Wife is ever about
you, my prayers often, very often in every day and
every night beseech our heavenly Father to shield,
comfort and direct you. For my own merit I can
ask nothing. Of His mercy and promises I can
hope every thing which it is expedient to bestow.
After faithful self examination it is permitted me
to say, I have not done to others as they do unto
me [*The period has been made from a comma here,
and the next words, equivalent to a line of writing, have
been crossed out by large black x's*]. There is no occasion now to make Frankensteins, like ready made

clothing they wait in abundance for customers. When Roberts grew angry with Byron you know he charged him with being miserable because of a soul of which he could not get rid. The Sentinel has stamped with such a noise back and forth in front of me, that I must cease from the effort to write until another and more quiet walker comes on, and I recover from the effect produced by the attempt to write under such difficulty—

My interruptions are not like your's of a character to afford a subject of pleasant reference and having long since come to regard them as not meant for my comfort it only remains to summon patience against them as evils from which it will be a virtue to extract good. I was very sorry to see that my early friend Hugh Mercer had been arraigned on a charge of murder. He cannot be guilty and surely must be acquitted, but to one of his gentle, generous nature it is a sad blow to be even thus unjustly accused. He was my class mate and I have always remembered him with tender affection, [*sic*] your letter gave me the first notice that Frank and B. were released.[13]

Somebody writing from Augusta to the Boston Advertiser, makes an extraordinary statement about a letter said to have been written to some one in Columbus by Mr. A.H. Stephens immediately after the Hampton Roads conference—containing the assertion that terms not humiliating to the South could be obtained, but that I and my principal advisers did not want peace. Of course Mr. S. could not have said any thing of the sort; as he had been twice employed to seek peace, and on the last occasion made a report written & oral, showing that no negotiation would be entertained. He was prepared to enlarge the written report by

the addition of such conclusions and impressions
as the confidential nature of a part of the conference would permit, but though the two other
commissioners appeared willing to do so, Mr. [*A.?*]
strongly objected, arguing that the bare recital of
facts was the best presentation of the case to the
public mind. Now as it would have been dishon-
est to conceal from me such an opportunity as is
described, and treacherous to the people to have
given such an account as it was thought would
most certainly lead them to the opposite conclusion. I take it that someone is slandering Mr.
Stephens, and so publicly, that even a philosopher
might be moved to correct it.—I saw the story
republished in the Tribune N.Y. about three weeks
ago. There has been certainly much zeal displayed
in the planting and cultivating of prejudice against
me, but many of the stories are so absurd that it
requires a morbid state of opinion to receive them.

The cochineal shirts were very opportune
and I have nightly used one since they came to
me. It was to me very apparent that they were
from the beloved hand that has so often soothed
my suffering and anticipated my wants. Nobody
else would have known the habit created by past
attention. The fervent pure prayers which went
up from the heart while the hand was working
may yet bring the appointed fruit; though after
many days. Should that moon be given to us,
even amid its pleasures I will as a duty mingle
many acknowledgments, for that or some other
opportunity more exclusive than this, I expec-
tantly wait.

"Dobbin" always was sterling, his Father and
his Mother were fine gold.[14] Tell him how gratefully I recognize his care for my children. Where

was the big boy on the 28th? How, what etc. x
x, as far as you know =. The credulity of exiles
once grew to a proverb.

I am truly thankful for the privilege of receiving with your's the letters of our little ones,
and will send to you an Answer to Maggie's addressed to her.

As Judge Speed has courteously forwarded
my child's letter addressed to me I presume he
will send to you the answer made in corresponding form. She asks for a lock of my hair and my
likeness, the hair I send the likeness I cannot
get. You will know how to arrange the hair for
her and will not wonder at the rudeness of my
attempt. Speaking of hair Ellen had probably
given that away to a woman in the neighborhood,
judging by the recital made to me. I should like
to know that girl who made the prompt application of Tennison [sic] to the Persimmon Tree.
This is the practical wisdom of the elder Mr.
Veller[15] I hope not to be as much mistaken in her
as I was in the one who recited without rests. It
was a mere guess of mine, when you read the
book you will observe the points which suggestin
[sic] that she might have become an authoress. I
wish all my mistakes were of persons who were
as little known, but on the whole it must be more
comfortable to be the deceived than the deceiver.
Sometimes I feel that there is a real compliment
in the trust displayed by some of my slanderers
to whom it must occur that with a single breath I
could topple over the miserable fabric their selfishness is making.

Jany 1st 1866—Though a heavy burden of oppression rests upon me and the prospect before is

gloomy in the extreme, my love undimmed sends it's greeting to you and my heart asks of our heavenly Father for a blessing on my sorrowing Wife and helpless little children. The year which opens with so little of promise to you may be like the bright day which follows the cloudy mornings; there is wisdom in borrowing comfort from the unknown future and it is reasonable to expect that which we feel to be just.

In the time when nations were ruled by arbitrary power, the Catholic Priests stood between the despots and their victims, sublimely defying the rage of one and divinely bending to raise the other. From time to time the heroic spirit of that ancient line has been called forth, and in plague, pestilence and famine; in the wilderness and on fields of blood; in the prison, on the scaffold and among the deserted mourners, nobly have they maintained the glory of their orders. In this light whoever views them will feel attracted to that one communion, and far be it from me to disparage the light which shines brightest in the storm that extinguishes the others. But the heroism that in the face of earthly peril continues in the line of duty to God, may have something of earth mingling with the truthful courage with commands esteem. The timid though he shrunk may have looked at the sufferer with longing love from the outer court. True at such a time it availed not, yet it might for other trials be all one wants.

If the letter to little Maggie reaches you please enclose it to her, if it does not tell her it was written and send her the hair—I am glad under any restraints to be able to write to you, and it is for me only to accept the terms which are imposed and leave others to judge whether they are properly observed. I should write more freely if I knew that the Atty. Genl. only inspected my letters, but as I send them open and don't know how they are forwarded, and do know that objections have been made here to the contents of a letter enclosed to the Atty. Genl. I have to conclude that they are read before they reach him, and may be stopped in the way. But this merely affects the mode of expression and to you who know my feelings so well nothing is less important than mere manner. Write as I may or if not at all, you will still know how truly I am, as these many years I have been, affetty[16]. your Husband.

[*in tiny letters*]
Mrs. Varina Davis   Jeffn Davis

Letter 12
(January 16-18, 1866)

[*The text of this page in the MS. is entirely over-written by the text of the last page at right angles, from bottom to top. For the wording, see the last page of this copy below.*]

Fortress Monroe Va.
16th Janry. 1866

Mrs. V. Davis.

My dear Wife, I have this day received yours of the 15th Ulto. with its enclosures. It does not surprise me that you were sad on the anniversary of a day, which with peculiar force brought to mind the separation of our family, and the sad causes which have led to it. Let us train our hearts to feel that these are afflictions given to direct us in the way that leads to eternal life. Thus, if we may not with joy accept the severe discipline, we may at least bear it with resignation. Our heavenly Father we are [*assured?*] does not chasten us in anger, but [*in love and?*] mercy; His instruments may be vengeful and unjust, as were those who murdered St. Stephen[1], but he looked beyond the rough rod

to the hand of the just and passionless Father
who held it, and though we may not attain to, we
should imitate that example.

I am truly distressed to hear of the death of
Miss Schley[2], her visit was known to me in a way
which increased my previous gratitude, but of the
catastrophe your letter gave the first information.
Her parents have my sincere sympathy, an offering
which is little worth, but the absence of which is
more regarded.

It seems to me that I know Mr. Wright, but
my reliance on a faculty which once served me
well is now down to zero. If however his kindness
was evoked by your helplessness only, I am not the
less, but the more grateful therefor. Victrix causa
Deis placuit, victa Catoni[3].

The condition of society as described in
Georgia is lamentable enough, and I fear it is
much the same generally in the planting states. It
is probable that our friend will find it worse, rather
than better in Texas.[4] He will not probably take his
family there before making a personal inspection.
Why do not well informed persons state the case
fully and truly to Presdt. Johnson, his knowledge
of the negro character and of the kind relations
which formerly existed between the slaves and
their masters, would enable him readily to perceive
the appropriate remedies for present disorders.
Though in view of the excitement and blindness
of the "Radicals" it may not be practicable to do
all which sound policy would otherwise dictate,
the worst grievances surely would be abated if
rightly understated. There cannot be many so fa-
natical that for the sake of keeping armed negroes
as a military police, they would render the lives of
white women and children insecure, and destroy

what little property the devastation of war has left.
However wisely conducted the transition of the
negro from his state of dependence to that of self
control, must involve serious difficulties; if speculative theory, experimenting without special information, is to direct the change, those to the manor
born will easily foresee the results. The resolute
will, calm temper and practical sense which seek to
extract good from unavoidable evil may if left un-
obstructed save enough from the wreck to prevent
the country from lapsing into desert. The efforts
now being made to import laborers may be finally
beneficial, but at first Europeans will be unskilled in
that agriculture, and must be acclimated before they
can be productive.

I had feared that our negroes would be disturbed by the introduction of others among them,
but could not have imagined that they would be
driven away from their home by those pretend-
ing to be their especial advocates. What a beast he
must have been who turned old Uncle Bob out of
his house, to find where he could a shelter for the
infirmities of more than a hundred winters. That
claim was manifest. Of the truth, the fidelity, the
piety which had so long secured him the respect
of all who knew him, a stranger might plead ignorance. Were one in proper position, to bring the
case to the notice of the authorities I cannot believe
such conduct would be tolerated. The chief of the
bureau[5] would probably correct it, as I understand
his policy has been to induce the negroes to remain
at their old homes. An agent suited to such work
would probably be able by proper representations to
remove the evils complained of at the H. & B.[6].

17th—I have been suffering from neuralgia in the

head and the usual effect upon the eyes causes me
to write at intervals. Do not be disturbed, the attack is not serious, indeed considering the circumstances, it is rather to be wondered at that I am not
worse. More that heretofore I use caution in all
things, so that my strength may be preserved for
whatever awaits me. Once a day it is still permitted
[*t's are not crossed*] to me to walk in the open air &
though the time is brief the result is beneficial.

I would be obliged to you for the suggested
shade for the eyes. Your ingenuity and handicraft
has so often come to my relief that hope always
hangs thereon. Since the attack of erysipelas my
nose has not been equal to the pressure of the
goggles. I have the pocket comb you put in a case
for me, so that you will have no occasion to attend to your offer in that regard. It is dear to me by
every mark and association.

Your Aunt Beulah's letter[7] is certainly re-
markable for one of her age; and is such as only
the good write. The place, and the employment at
the time of the writing are significant. Did it strike
you that there is evidence in the [*style (Intl.)*] that
she has come to think in German. In a former letter I mentioned that the arrest of J.D.H[8] had probably been made by mistake as to his identity, but if
the account be fully given, it is a case of such false
imprisonment as cannot fail if properly prosecuted
to obtain redress. In that region the civil courts
have power, and will hardly overlook robbery as
the attendant of unwarrantable arrest. Thank you
for Maggie's letter and Jefferson's copy—your
telegram to Genl. Miles gave me relief—greater
that I care to express. With you I am thankful for
the guidance which led our persecuted children
to a refuge, not only from the dangers which sur-

rounded them, but from the condition in which
their education could not be properly advanced.
It is an unfailing consolation to know that they
are doing so well, but my anxiety remains that
you should have supervision of them, and I hope
you will soon be allowed to depart and join them.
You have watched long for the coming of good
news in regard to me, but have watched in vain!
The many months which have elapsed open no
brighter view; bad news travels fast and will reach
you soon enough wherever [*written at end of line:*
"whereever"] you may be. I suppose the privilege of
correspondence will remain as now, and though I
will not assume to be above the influence of increasing distance, or expect you to be so; duty to
our children claims preference over even the tenderest sentiment. All the forms of the duty to be
performed will occur to you, with their embar[r]
assments [*hindrances*] and responsibilities. It is not
desirable that I should now discuss them. I will
only add that I hope my Wife and children will
[*except as deprived by due process of law, (Intl.)*] receive for their support either my property or my
personal services.

There can be no plausible ground for with-
holding J.E.D's property from him and if he
would engage the attention of the authorities at
Washington the restoration would surely not be
delayed. The reply of Watson makes an issue with
the clerk and I think the latter will meet it properly.[9]

Did you, for me, acknowledge Ellen's letter
forwarded by you some time since? Please give
her my warmest affection when you write to her.
The account she gives of our relations['] anxiety
concerning me adds another to my many burdens

of grief. Tell Brother Joe. that he need not fear on
account of the one source of his apprehension. I
hope he will soon be relieved of his recent vexa-
tions, and that it may be my fortune to meet him
again in this world; and if I can do no more, at
least to relieve him of the painful solicitude he
suffers on my account. I do not understand the
wanderings of Fannie's Joe and feel apprehensive
concerning him. Does he write to you? The offer to send the children's photographs was generous, but I can imagine or rather remember very
distinctly how they looked when we parted, and
will not deprive you of these, if I do not see them
before they have greatly changed you can send me
others to show their new appearance. Until then
they will assemble as above, heretofore.[10] It was
unfeeling to recite to you the suspicion that Becket
was the person; but you couldn't expect a bowl to
be free from evaporation when in the exhausted
receiver of its own thoughts; or to be empty when
just brought in from a shower of gossip. The impression so injudiciously recited in[11] regard to
myself was that most likely to be received by one
engaged in an attempt to discriminate in favor of
another. It is one of the proofs of a special Providence that agents seem to be moulded for the work
they are to perform, and if the work be good we
can overlook the defects which fit the agent for it.
For example high sensibility, unyielding candor
and pure principles would have been unsuited to
it's task [*Babble is not so harmful as railing though it be
of the mean kind* (*Intl.*)].

In the same train of thought I will remark
that whether the offences noticed in "errata"
against courtesy were the result of ignorance or
of insolence, they had no value unless they should

be noticed. In the first case the shaft was sent unconsciously, in the second being disregarded the rebuke would be felt which the meanest must feel, contempt so complete as to be silent. As to the individual even supposing him to be moved by the motives ascribable logically to his conduct, he is but on a parity with other and more prominent men, some of whom when they read their high eulogiums, not unfrequently bestowed, and think of their [(*Intl. in small script*) *past relations to myself and their moral responsibility at least equal to mine*] must in that praise taste the bitterest gall; unless as Genl. Washington said of Arnold, they are too base for remorse. Their temerity shows I have not lost their confidence & they have my pity.—persecuted though I be for a creed they held in common with me, when it's advocacy promised favor instead of odium, preferment instead of sacrifice & my danger; I can from the depth of my misfortune look down with pity on their selfishness.

18th—The newspapers will have informed you of events at Washington, for obvious reasons I will make no comment, save to point you to the unavoidable conclusion that you can no longer cherish the hope which was formerly indulged. Strengthen your heart for the high responsibilities imposed on you & go forward on the path of duty, accepting every providence with the comforting assurance that it must be right. Truth is powerful and the common sense of justice recoils, after the paroxysm of passion subsides, from continuance in wrong doing. Then I say, of the final result of any proceeding against me, be hopeful; my conduct has been too public, too consistent to be perverted, after slanderers are confronted by true witnesses. It is hard for me to be reconciled to the trials to which my Wife and little children are exposed, but I trustingly pray that God will hide them under the shadow of his wings until earth's calamities are overpast.

I will be glad when you are removed beyond the reach of the brutal cruelty of such statements and suggestions as those which have so disturbed you. They are crosses which you cannot bear and I have seen [(*Intl.*) *in your letters*] their evil as well as painful effect upon you. By dwelling they grow into more than [(*Intl.*) *their*] real importance. It was to remove a stumbling block that I referred to the parable, but from your answers perceive that my treatment was injudicious and regret the error. The gifts [(*Intl.*) *with which men are divinely endowed*] are various, and the requirements of the Lord are never beyond the range of possibility; for He knows our infirmities and judges of our motives. These man cannot know and is therefore forbidden to judge. We hope [(*Intl.*) *& pray*] for [(*Intl.*) *God's*] forgiveness on the ground of true repentance, and as we cannot tell in the case of those who trespass against us, whether the repentance is true or feigned, we are bound to accept the seeming. That is possible, is it not easy, for virtue far short of the God like or saintly examples of the Redeemer and the first Christian martyrs? I struggle, not always successfully, against my temptations, and often feel how much communion with you, would aid my efforts to walk in the way of the Fathers [*sic*] commandments.

[The rest of this letter is found written perpendicular to the script already comprising the first page of this letter These are the last words of the would-be last page of this

*letter. Now begins the overwriting which is explained
in the note at the top of the letter. The first word is very
faint, but seems to be "In." The overwritten text goes
on:*]

my isolation a daily experience enables me to realize the heart warming influence of little Winnie's
presence with you and [*illegible word*] thinking of
her enables me to imagine her growth and progress. She is most associated in my mind with the
memory of Sister Ann[12] and the sadness which
Ellen described confusedly mingles with thoughts
of the child. Kiss the little angel for me. Did she
keep her baby, tear it up or lose it? Farewell dear
Wife there is a great satisfaction in feeling that you
know most of that which I would write but do not.
And it is perhaps fortunate that the restraint exists
as it is one of the pressures upon feelings which
it is necessary for me to control by every means
within my power. [*Faint word, perhaps "Oh"*] May
He that will not break a bruised reed, guide and
comfort you Your loneliest hour will not be alone,
for there is no emotion which does [*not?*] send my
spirit to hover about the object of its dearest affection. Again dear Wife farewell. Your Husband

Jeffn Davis

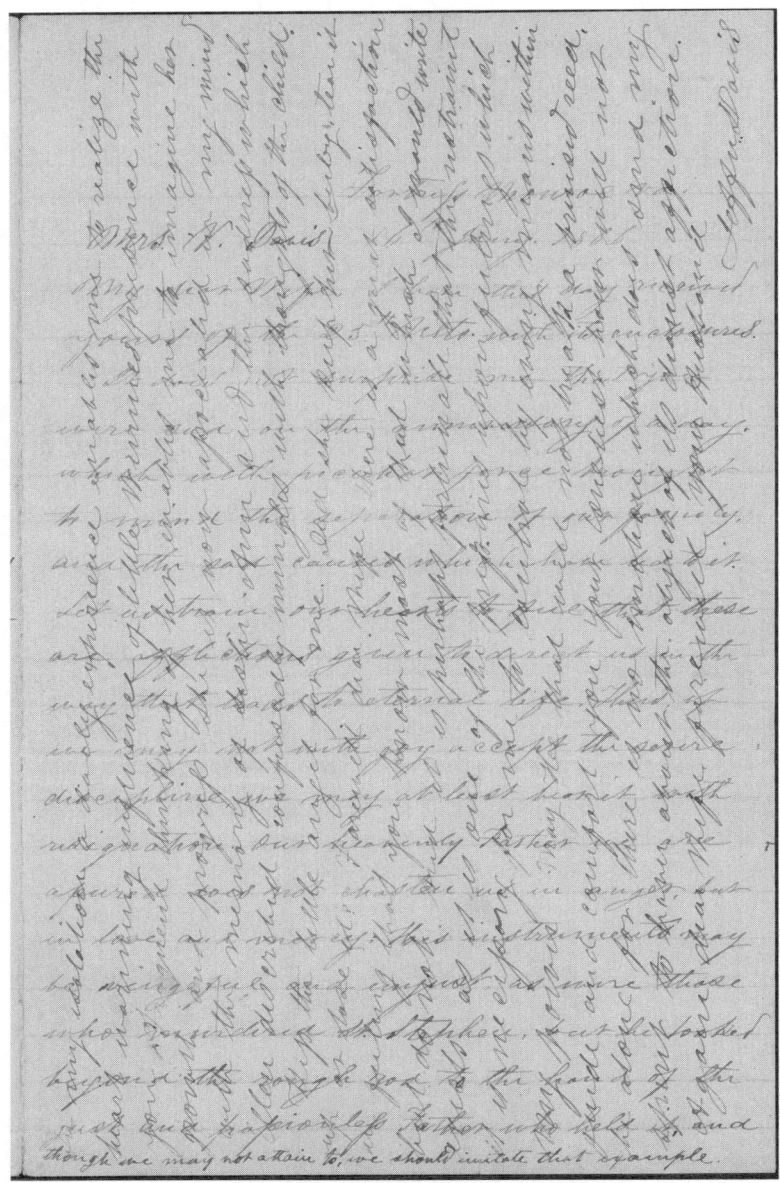

Page 1 of Letter 12 (*January 16-18, 1866*).

I will be glad when you are removed
beyond the reach of the brutal cruelty of such
statements and suggestions as those which
have so disturbed you. They are crosses which
you cannot bear and I have seen in your letters, their evil
as well as painful effect upon you. By dwelling
on them, they grow into more than their real importance.

It was to remove a stumbling block that I
referred to the parable, but from your answer
perceive that my treatment was injudicious,
and regret the error. The gifts with which men are divinely endowed are various, and
the requirements of the Lord are never beyond
the range of possibility; for He knows our infirmities and judges of our motives. These
man cannot know, and is therefore for-
bidden to judge. We hope a pray for God's forgiveness on the
ground of true repentance, and as we cannot
tell in the case of those who trespass against
us, whether the repentance is true or feigned,
we are bound to accept the seeming. That is
possible, it not easy, for virtue far short of the
God like or saintly examples of the Redeemer
and the first Christian martyrs I struggle, not
always successfully against my temptations, and often
feel how much communion with you, would aid my
efforts to walk in the way of the Father's commandments.

Page 2 of Letter 12 (*January 16-18, 1866*).

Letter 13
(January 24-26, 1866)

Fortress Monroe Va. 24 Jany 66

My dear Wife,

Your's of the 12th Inst. is received and I comply with your request for prompt answer as my
circumstances have permitted. The photograph
which you mention as enclosed was not found
with the letter. Was it sent. [*sic*] If it had occurred
to me at the time I would have put a larger lock
of hair in little daughter's letter, will remedy the
failure by enclosing another in this. The manuscript[1] and printed enclosure came safely with
your letter. You attach over much importance to
the publication made of your letter. Those who
know you will need no assurance that it was not
written with such expectation, and no one will
find any thing in it inconsistent with a proper
feeling or inappropriate to the occasion. The relation you bear to the people of Missi is sufficiently
stated to be understood by those who were not
previously informed, and the difference between
the offering of a multitude, and donation of an

individual is generally recognized as satisfactory to pride, a sentiment which has not the most intimate connection with logic.

I thought William was in Europe but from a passage in your letter infer it was a mistake—and that together with his Sister and baby being with her Mother makes the whole situation quite unintelligible and not most pleasantly suggestive.[2] If your supposition in regard to the illness of M. is correct there was a strange misapprehension in the diagnosis. Dobbin will be able to give you exact information in regard to the children, after which you will be better able to decide whether they should wait for your coming to them or not. I like their present condition the less for recent changes, and as you know only contented myself because of the necessity for the arrangement which was made. I cannot conceive of a pretext for keeping you in Georgia and would suggest that you get some one to make the application for you, so as to remove the difficulty if there be one in replying to you directly. When you join the children go with them to some place where you can be isolated, and sufficiently off of the thoroughfares to escape from newsmongers and to avoid the cholera. In regard to the latter, I have confidence in Cartwright's treatment[3] and in the exemption of places on primitive rock. You will remember the advantages of using rain water—

Do not allow the hope of being permitted to visit me to influence your action. The children are now in that impressible state that receives for good or evil impressions from every object with which they are in contact. The words spoken before a child, as too small to hear and understand, are often noted and long remembered; the example of irreverence, violence, or wrangling may change the whole character; as indulgence of idleness, or appetite or wayward temper in matters so small as to be forgotten, may lay the foundation of both negative and positive views. If I should regain my liberty I will go to you; and in the mean time you will be employed in the way which will best promote the children's welfare and our happiness.

Your question about the Smith's[4] involves so many considerations of fact and law, that it is impossible for me to give an answer. The old man was sensible and of strong will, what the young ones are I cannot say. Ignorance or dishonesty might equally explain their course; and to one or both it must be referred. If the labor could be at once employed and the requisite money provided, [*the next word is "The" or "She" with two dots over the "e" and the text goes on:*] could ascertain about the title etc., etc. from some of the Lawyers there— say Hooker or Wharton. The letter you cite may have been written after inquiry and reflection if so it will suffice as to the law. If the transaction is safe, and The[5] can see how it is to be done I would deem it better than reversion without release. You ask me to be explicit, forgetting how little I know of the present condition of affairs. You will see at least that the effort has been made to do more than merely plead inability to decide, and you will write according to your better knowledge of events, conferring with J.E.D. or [*illegible word*] not as you choose. It must be hard for you to realize [*illegible word*] completely I am shut out from all knowledge of what is passing except as revealed in such papers as are permitted to reach me, being numbers of a few least friendly. The night and morning watches are by the author of the "Faithful Promiser".[6] [*They*] were published by the "Protestant Episcopal Society"[7] at New York. It is not possible for me to get and send it to you, as I once would have done.

I can readily realize the timidity that restrains men of truth from speaking boldly and suppose there are restraints upon the publication of views in the Southern papers, but think it probable that Genl. Lee like myself did not know how he had been referred to by Mr. Colfax. It would not have withdrawn him long from other duties to have opposed a statement so utterly devoid of truth and I cannot doubt the pleasure it would have given him to do so, unless indeed he considers it too absurd for belief. Judge Campbell I have been told wrote a full account of the interview with Mr. Lincoln and Mr. Seward, and that it had been published in the Northern papers. Mr. Hunter[8] promised me to write such a statement. The stories told of Mr. Stephens[9] are improbable because the meanest capacity must perceive, that my powers and duties rested in the organization made by the Southern States, and that it would have been treasonable usurpation to attempt to destroy the organization by the existence of functions given to maintain it. When the Continental Congress sent commissioners to meet Lord Howe, who had announced himself as empowered to treat for the adjustment of the controversy between the States and G Britain[10], the Commissioner on learning that the basis must be a return to allegiance, informed his Lordship that the colonies having declared their Independence, it was not competent for the Congress to return them to a state of dependence. In both cases there was an obvious mode, but it was adopted in neither, to suspend hostilities and

submit propositions to be laid before the states.
Judge Campbell made an inquiry which opened,
and received an answer which closed that view. I
suppose it is narrated in his statement. Excluded
from an opportunity to reply slanders have worked
without check and have no doubt deceived many.
Again, any dolt whose blunders required frequent
correction and whose vanity sought for some one
on whom to lay the responsibility of his failures,
could readily, and if man enough would now, ascribe them to me. Things done against my known
views, and of which explanations were written
to me when success was expected to result from
the change of plan, have lately been attributed to
my orders—Beauregard, Hood, Hardee and Cobb
know of a case in point, memorable by its consequences.[11]

Genls. Lee and Bragg could give the history
of the two largest armies and it is due to truth that
they should do it, whenever circumstances will
permit. I never sought to make up my own record,
intent on the discharge of my duties in the various
public positions I have held, if the question had
occurred to me how will this be told hereafter, I
would have preferred to leave that talk to others.
Nor is the hazard great for the dependence of the
parts of a whole, will generally correct the perver-
sions of recital by interested narrators.

That power to compare and sift testimony is
as necessary to a historian as to an attorney, and I
hope the faculty will be put in exercise proportionate to the field our times has [sic] offered.

Recurring to that hill place[12], if your confinement was to Missi. it might serve for shelter and
employment. It is as healthy as any in that region
and better than most others for cultivation so far as

my cursory observation enabled me to judge. The
N.Y. papers containing an account of the interview between the South Ca[13] committee and Presdt. Johnson was handed to me soon after its publication. I did not credit the statement because I was
sure you had not in such a correspondence given
expression to your personal feelings; nor [*several
words obliterated*] if from the fullness of the heart of
an agonized Wife and Mother pleading for the restoration of those dearest objects of her love, you
had written what might have been better omitted,
did it seem to me probable that the Presdt. would
have referred to it as was reported. I hoped you
would never see the publication and did not myself feel willing to write of that, which I could not
remedy or even examine. Neither of us have [*sic*]
probably learned the philosophy of Uriah Heap[14]
but there is dignity as well as policy in abstaining
from ineffectual complaint. The apprehensions
you express as to indications of legislation of an
ex-post facto character so as to give additional
assurance of a conviction in my case, are not
unreasonable, and taken in connection with other
disclosures of purpose led me in my last letter to
you, to advise you to abandon the hope you had
so fondly indulged of an early opportunity to see
me. To all the trials mental and physical to which
I am subjected I will oppose all the moral power
I possess that my life may be prolonged as far as
such drains will permit and my power to meet any
future ordeal be as great as possible to me. Mrs.
Clay returned to this place yesterday [*and*] is today
with her Husband again—She applied for permission to visit me but it was not granted. Mr. Clay
has not been well as usual lately. Like myself he
no doubt suffers from food unsuited to him, and to

anyone in close confinement I think it would soon become so. His friends in Va. have given him some relief occasionally and his Wife will no doubt have a basket full of consolation. Mrs. C. is I hear to return to Washington before going home and expects to be here again, in two or three weeks.

[*The following script appears upside-down in the empty space at the top of this letter's first page:*] My letters are all enclosed in one envelope addressed to you, which is placed in another addressed to Atty. Genl. Speed. [*Beneath this appears, on the left in even smaller script:*] 26 Jan'y. 66 [*and on the right:*] J.D.

Letter 14
(January 28-29, 1866)

F. Monroe. Va.—28th Jany 66

My dear Wife,

Your's of the 17 Inst., with the photograph
is received. I am grateful for both, though I cannot say that the likeness is satisfactory and it is a
poor specimen of art. The process is necessarily
a caricature and therefore suited only to a certain cast of features & complexion. Neither of us
belong [*sic*] to that class. It serves me, however the
pleasant means of comparison with the two previously in possession. This is another one which is
not carried in the pocket, not to be seen of others,
and of fadeless tints, which is better than all of
these. That one can neither be destroyed or stolen,
it shines by its own light, is always present and
visible. I like others but do not need them, and
am not satisfied with them; they cannot have the
expression which is only given to one who well
understands but cannot translate it. Mrs. Clay is
still here and as I learn daily visits her Husband.
I am indebted to her for several kind attentions in
the way of comestibles and for a photograph of

herself in evening dress. The fact of her Husband's continued stay here shows the failure of her main purpose in visiting Washington City. But her visit is said to have benefited her Husband who as mentioned in my last letter has not been recently as well as usual. The regret which you felt in reading of the privileges she enjoyed that you were not equally indulged is fully realized by me, but let me warn you against the picture your imagination paints by drawing it's hues from memory. The scenes you recall could not be renewed here. Instead of the quiet and freedom and comfort the surroundings would be wounding to your sensibility and pride. Be comforted at least in this that you lose less than your imagination sketched. It is too hard for me to bear the discrimination made against us alone of all similarly situated, not to render me duly sensible of the anguish you feel but my dear Wife lift up your heart in the confidence that all our afflictions are to fit us for a better state, and to secure to us a reunion which shall never cease.

I had supposed that the failure to obtain permission to go to the children might have resulted from causes which it was not desirable to state to you, therefore in a former letter I suggested that you should make the application through some one at Washington. Thinking it probable that you might know better than myself who could and would thus serve you I did not name any one. If I had done so it would probably have been a Senator who[m] I have from my childhood remembered with affection, to whom I would have given whatever friendship could claim, and of whose manhood I could not have felt a doubt but I recently saw a newspaper paragraph which described him

as voluntarily joining in the detraction which my
misfortune not only permits but seems to excite.
So that you must use your better information
of the present temper of persons in selecting an
agent. Make no conditions precedent, you will
not be permitted to serve me and recent events
but impress even to the degree of a necessity, the
importance of your presence with the children.
The proposition of M.[1] is to me a sad disappointment. I had regarded the trip there as a high resolve to supply your place, and if the associations
are such as to make a withdrawal wished for, how
was it reconcilable to leave the children to such
influences. The proposition however carried with
it its answers, by showing that the expectation was
not well founded and that you have no substitute.
If you will be permitted only to go as an exile,
then so go. Gather the children around you and
separate yourselves as the best lights you receive
may guide you. If you are to be kept as a prisoner
among a people only connected by the sympathy
created by the harshness of your treatment, then
you had probably better accept the offer of the
Bishop, and send Billy to Fannie until your condition is changed, <u>provided</u> your information assures
you of safety there from such dangers as required
the removal of the children from Savannah, and
subject to the information you get from Dobbin on
his promised visit. If the third point proves inad-
missible could he not go with the Big boy and be
located near his school until old enough to enter
it. If this be better and Robert has not deteriorated
he could both serve and protect. There is one more
supposition i.e. that if permitted to go to Missi.
you should as soon as the state of the country
gains assurance of safety that you should have

the children brought to you there, that you may cling together supporting and supported until the cloud shall have passed. If in reading this it seem to you hard so was the struggle in which I spent the night and the cheerless anguish with which I met the coming day. Torture of myself, indignity and danger to myself I can meet and bear, would that my helpless family were spared. Too partially informed of current events to reason upon them as causes tending to certain results, and recognizing the liability to have my views colored by the somber shadows of my situation, I will not utter the gloomy forebodings which the course pursued by the Congress has created. The circle was an ancient symbol to express perfected change, a like idea is contained in the familiar expression that history repeats itself, and in the Biblical form, what has been shall be[2], each and all contain a sad warning. Fierce as was the strife of the French Revolution, the most violent passions were developed after the strife had ceased, for then the blood shedding passed from the cruel sword to the more cruel gown, from the necessities of the battle field to the vindictiveness of the party. The horrors of San Domingo did not originate in hostility of races, but in the speculative "philosophy" of men so remote that they could have but a nebulous observation of the bodies whose movements they undertook to "reform." Dr. Cartwright when in Paris traced the nefarious scheme to its true source and corrected the errors on which so much theory had been founded. If emissaries working at first secretly could so disturb social organism, what could not a lodge of men with power to decide all questions affecting a class with which they were identified effect Here will be the laborer complaining that he is robbed or defrauded, there the employer pledging similar wrongs. But if the body of officials be not courts there will be no appeal or if there be the officials not being Lawyers they will hardly have records intelligible to the legal profession. But I have said more than was designed or perhaps necessary to the conclusion; that I wish you with the children to seek some refuge where you will have not only safety but security, to the end that you may train them to the self denial, self reliance and perseverance which will render them a comfort and support to your old age.

I am not unmindful of your straitened circumstances but it did not seem to me that the course suggested in the last sentence would fail to diminish your expenses below the amount now required. Neither am I unobservant of your remark as to the failure of your past efforts to obtain permission to go to your children but have written under the hope that the permission will not be long withheld and if any of the remarks are now inapplicable they may be considered when circumstances shall have made them appropriate.

Brother Joe cannot protect the negroes against those public officers of whom they complain, and will only involve himself in controversy most unequal and vexatious. I wish he would employ an agent who would have less personal feeling for the negroes and therefore more prudence in defending them; and go himself with Lize[3] to some place where he could be more quiet and comfortable. The negroes know how promptly he would sympathize with them if imposed on and may have magnified their wrongs, most people will, and they always did, in times when I knew them, expand their narratives beyond the limit of the paper cover. Poor creatures they may well cry out to be saved from their "friends" so self-called. If they could bring an officer of the Bureau[4] before a civil court the law making them competent witnesses would have the protective effect which was its chief recommendation, when we used to discuss the question in the olden time. Hamlet's aunt had no doubt considered the world, but the negative form of the proposition as it is put in Fannie Kemble's Francis I is I think more exact; it excludes all which is not, but does not necessarily include all which is. You may recollect the tribute paid in the memoirs of the Baroness De Reidesel to Genl. Schuyler who received her when she came to the Hd. Qrs. of Genl. Gates following her Husband who with Genl. Burgoyne had been conducted there after their surrender. Did you ever hear that Col. MaCree refused to dine with the Duke of Wellington. He of course gave no reason on that occasion, but it was well understood to be on account of the treatment received by Napoleon after his surrender. In the case of Hampton[5], Hamlet's aunt would not have found an exception and I hope the wave that rolled heavily over him will have left the power to recover from the shock and that he may have the good fortune he richly deserves. I was surprised to see the name of Mr. Yulee among the political prisoners still kept in close confinement and the more I have thought of it the more it surprises me that such a result was obtained by comparison.

Much that it is [*sic*] now hidden will I hope be revealed even in this world and the honest, consistent, true lovers of constitutional principles will receive their reward, though they may suffer long after hypocrisy and false pretenses have relieved others from all save the reproaches of their own conscience, if indeed such people have not disposed of that restraint as Peter Schemyl did of his shadow[6]. Not the least sad of the consequences of civil wars is the moral decadence which usually follows. I could but expect your deep interests would make you an attentive observer but must regret that it has made you so acute to preserve the signs of the times.

It is not long since a newspaper paragraphist would have been rebuked by public opinion if he had attempted by epithets and one-sided statements to inflame the mind of his readers against a prisoner waiting a trial, but that would have been a small offense compared with that of a law maker who would seek to produce that effect and then by retrospective legislation to bring it to bear upon an anticipated trial such prejudiced minds with the power to judge. The speech to which you referred[7] is an extraordinary accumulation of reprehensible innovations. The minor objections growing out of the official character of the person[8] which if alone would be great are hidden by the magnitude of the offense of uttering such libelous assertion under the circumstances which he knew surrounded me. That his authority was not called for, that he was not scoffed by the multitude as the home bred sentiment of fair play demanded, shows you how deep seated the disease has become. The same conclusion as to your course is reached by every line of thought. Trying as it may be, you will have to make the effort to leave me, for the present, out of all your plans and may our Heavenly Father strengthen your heart for the difficult task of filling the place of both parents to our children. Tarry thou the Lord's pleasure[9] and let us always remember that all He does is right and that here after it will be given to us to comprehend his ways and say all was well. I hoped you would not see as plainly as you have, coming events and have avoided explicit expression lest I should give you pain. The departure from that practice has been so disagreeable to me, that I will here stop and try to ease my aching head by sleep.

29th—Lord "cause me to hear thy loving kindness in the morning, for in thee do I trust".[10] What a blessed promise that is for those who like ourselves cannot actually assemble together which is contained in Matt. XVIII. 19[11]—but we must remember always to take it in the spiritual sense of the New Testament.

An officer of the garrison of this place, informed me that he is a cousin of Mr. Hathaway, who he said is teaching school near to his Father's house and proposes to practice law after a time. He said H. had pretty much run through his property by idleness, spoke well of him otherwise and expressed for him a <u>brotherly affection</u>. Mrs. Clay had told him wherewithal induced the conversation.—of her statement I know only that H. was mentioned as having been with me.[12]

From you only do I learn any thing in relation to my dear relatives in Mi. & La. You will not require to be told how anxious I am concerning them and how depressing was the intelligence concerning the state of affairs at Locust Grove[13] compelling removal to the city for safety. Oh! that the law makers had facts instead of fictions on which to base their action in regard to the Southern States.

Please give expression as you will know how to my feelings for my little Pollie Big Boy and Button whenever you write and when which I hope will be soon you see them. Kiss "ittie Pie Davy for me and tell her until she understands how dearly I love her and how I long to hold her in my arms. I miss the development of her speech but yet I realize it from your vivid descriptions and my concentrated thoughts. My own Winnie fear not what men can do, it is God disposes.[14] Now I am shut up[15] and slander runs riot to destroy my fair repute, but any investigation must redeem my character and leave it for an inheritance to my children of which in after times they will not be the worse for possessing. The treatment I have received will be compared with my treatment of others and it will be the reversal of the picture my enemies have drawn. Let my discharge of Brownlow[16] on the plea of good faith be contrasted with my pursuit and arrest in a district where military operations were to be stopped. You know I believe the circumstances of the first named case, you certainly do, the events in the latter and I will not tell again either tale. Conscious rectitude is a great support to the sufferer whatever may be the form or the end of the afflictions. You will make the due allowance for my conditional expression of opinion in regard to all outside affairs, and for the prolixity which incertitude begets. Your better information will enable you to correct errors and to perceive remedies not known of to me [*sic*]. It is a great consolation to me that I can safely trust to your head as well as your heart.

Though my letter is very long my mind suggests many things which I would like to write,but they must be postponed to some occasion when you have not been so heavily taxed, and I am urged to close lest this should not be in time for today's mail. Farewell my much long loved Wife. Every hope, every pain every speculative thought whether of organic or inorganic bodies brings to me the want of your presence.

Do not lose the advantage you have of communion with others to turn your thoughts from the sad memory of our separation.

May the Lord shield and guide you, give you that grace which sanctifies every trial and cheers the thorny way with the blessed hope that it was chosen by Him as that which would best bring us to His fold. Once more dearest Winnie farewell, all of love unspoken your heart will suggest as felt by mine—Ever affectionately praying for our reunion in peace and safety I am

Your Husband

Jeffn. Davis [*written rather large*]

Mrs. Varina Davis

Letter 15
(February 3-4, 1866)

[*In this margin, perpendicular to the text, left to right, is the message*:] Awkwardly done, but you can reform it.

Fortress Monroe, Va.
3^d Feby 1866

Mrs. Varina Davis

My dear Wife,

Again I greet my best consolatory visitor, another letter from you, dated Jany. 22^d "66. One only who can realize the torturing anxiety with which each day after day I prayed to know what was passing with you, during the time when you were not permitted to write to me, can measure the support which is given to me by your letters. My heart longs for your presence, yearns for restoration to my children and reason urges the advantage to us all of such reunion. My love of my country is intensified by the knowledge of its distress and the partial knowledge I possess of the condition of public affairs leads me constantly to work out solutions which perhaps have suggested themselves to others, have been found to be impracticable, and therefore not adopted. It is however generally true of controversies, that those who look on from a distance see more clearly than the contestants. Passion rises with the struggle and obscures and distorts the mental vision as the dust and smoke of the battlefield does that of the eye. Thus men turn to the judgement of posterity for the reversal of the decrees of their contemporaries, appealing with the self-sustaining hope of conscious rectitude, from "Phillip drunk to Phillip sober."

Mr. Minnigerode[1] visited me yesterday and left me with a promise to come again in a fortnight, as he had obtained permission to visit regularily [sic]. He said his request to that effect had been very courteously granted and I am thankful not only for the renewed visit but for the greater freedom allowed to the interview.

You have been causelessly disturbed by the report you mention in regard to the manner of confinement. I am in the same room as heretofore and no change has been made in my condition in it. The story of a rescue to be made by men coming one at a time on coasting vessels was so ridiculous to any one acquainted with this place and its garrison arrangements, that I cannot suppose it was ever seriously regarded by any one here. Those who might be willing in a manner which rendered success possible, to risk themselves for me, would foresee the evil consequences to our people, and would not fail to do me the justice to remember, that I would much rather be a sacrifice for the country than it should be sacrificed for me.

The news papers will have informed you

of the petition in my behalf by seven thousand Ladies of Richmond and vicinity. It was not in-effectual, it refreshed my burdened heart as the shower revives a parched field; if it avail nothing elsewhere it has been a blessing to me; and I may hope as I pray, that He who judges the heart of man and requires love and mercy, will requite their goodness according to their need.

Connected with the idea of a Providential requital of deeds in kindness done, I will mention an incident related to me a few days since by an officer on duty with the present garrison. He said his Mother told him that when she was an orphan child in the charge of her Aunt whose husband resided in a village on the northern frontier where I was then serving as a Lieut. of Infantry, that her nurse treated her cruelly, and that on one occasion when I was on a visit to the villages the nurse had her out and was whipping her, that I interposed for her protection and reported the case to her Uncle in-law, so as to have the nurse dismissed, by which she was relieved from future harshness—was I not rewarded by the instrumentality of that man who saved my little daughter from the negro sentinel in Savannah? My brain burns when I think of the brute leveling his musket at my little, gentle child. Father, protect my helpless family, beneath thy wings give them shelter until the storm has passed. Oh! faithful Shepherd, take these stricken lambs in thy loving arms and bear them to thy "paths of pleasantness and peace"[2].

I have just heard that Mr. Cass[3] is dieing [*sic*], and regret it as well on account of my kind feeling for him and the respect which amicable character commanded as because [*sic*] he was one of those on whom I felt I could rely to vindicate my charac-

ter from some of the accusations made against me,
after Mr. Crittenden there was not one to whom
I talked so much and so freely concerning the
sectional troubles in 1860-1. With Mr. Crittenden
I daily conferred when we served on the Compromise committee[4] in that winter; the record of
which shows who it was who opposed every effort
at accommodation.

Mr. Buchannan[5] [*sic*] in his book has verified
the judgement of his Pennsylvania acquaintance
who ascribed to him vindictiveness as his absorb-
ing trait. I then thought they were unjust but must
admit as it was their wont to say, that they knew
him better than I did. While employing argument
to convict Genl. Scott of an offence and rhetoric
to intensify its heinousness he commits against
me the very extreme of which he accuses Genl.
S. When he says southern Senators and especially
Jefferson Davis became alienated because of his
annual message of 1860, who would imagine that
the criticism of the especial J.D. had been made to
the writer on the rough draft of his message and in
such friendly spirit as to lead to several modifica-
tions. That the known relations between us had
caused two of his cabinet to send me an urgent
dispatch to come immediately to Washington
when the Message was in course of preparation.
And that after the Message had been delivered,
repeated conferences between us were held in
regard to affairs in South Carolina, etc. At last being made painfully aware that I had been treated
with unfairness and put in a false position by using
assurances given to me, as a means of restrain-
ing others; I did, and therefore did, terminate all
friendly intercourse; though even as late as the
receipt of the telegrams giving an account of the

firing on the Star of the West, I went to him and made another effort to induce him to adopt a line of action which seemed to me most likely to avoid collision and to give the best prospect for a peaceful solution. I hope he has forgotten much, and only wish his memory had been better or worse. He retained the telegrams for the purpose of taking copies, to be used in a proposed Cabinet meeting & returned them.

As my memory serves me, his Message of 1860 had a great deal to commend it and in ordinary times that which was most objected to, by southern men, would have been dismissed as a discussion upon terms, verbology. Censure so unreasonable has pursued the old man in his retirement, that I had come to remember the good to the exclusion of the evil, I wish he had left me that pleasure.

I saw recently and with sincere gratification that Mr. Pierce had been confirmed in the Episcopal Church. A true hearted gentleman, an honest statesman, a zealous patriot, a gallant soldier, a faithful friend, a generous foe, in public and private relations of pure principles, of clear head, consistent conduct and nice honor, I am proud to have been associated closely with him and happy to believe that he still remembers me with friendship though it has been many years since I have heard from him.[6]

Like you I feel sorry for the negroes, what has been done would gradually and measurably be corrected by the operation of the ordinary laws governing the relation of labor to capital if they were left alone, but interference by those who have a theory to maintain by the manufacture of facts must result in evil, evil only and continually. At every assertion that the Southern people hate the negroes my surprise is renewed, but a hostility not now or heretofore existing between the races may be engendered by just such influences as are indicated. Only personal feeling would prevent a land owner from avoiding the meddling of a bureau agents [*sic*], by substituting former slaves by white laborers. With these contracts could be made; crops gathered and disposed of without the annoyance and tax of the Middleman, to say nothing of the dangers of his jurisdiction.

There are natural laws in morals as well as in physics and he who violates them may be expected to reap as he who sows the wind, how many people in the reforming, amending days, play the part of Mrs. Clark on the Steam Boat. She was not permitted to try her moral plan of navigation, would that the parallel may continue.

Dr. Craven I learn is in the neighborhood, but it has not been my good fortune to see him since he was relieved from duty at this post. Mr. Leonard is again in Norfolk[7], has an intelligence office, is still lame—and this was all I could learn. Mrs. Clay has gone to Washington City & expected to return here on her way to the South in some ten or twelve days. If you should see her she could no doubt give you much news of the persons she met but little if any thing on the one subject of which you would wish to hear. The "notions" afloat about the capitol are of such specific gravity that one could carry any quantity of them, and you know their value in times more sedate than these, therefore could not think a basket of such ware worth the unpacking. The dim distance hides all the proportions of the future and I can only hope that you will be able to address yourself to current demands upon you, and we will unite in asking for that which if it be expedient[8] our Lord will in due time grant to our joint prayer.

[*Now we find the explanation of JD's marginal note on page 1*:] I have endeavored to comply exactly with your wish in regard to the hair and will stitch it to the first page after tying it as directed. Mr. Minnigerode promised me to send to you the Morning and Night Watches[9] and I hope they may please you as much as they have me. Since the time when mention was made of my suffering from neuralgia of the head, and dyspepsia the latter has been diminished by more proper diet and the former has subsided even more rapidly. Again let me urge you not to allow yourself to be disturbed by rumors in relation to me, they are so unreliable that you could not believe them if favorable and should not be distressed at those which are otherwise. On the night of the thirtieth I was sitting before the fire because I could not sleep and had a startling optical illusion, such you know as were common in fever; but to my vision, I saw little Pollie walk across the floor and kneel down between me and the fire in the attitude of prayer, I moved from consequent excitement and the sweet vision melted away. I have not called it a dream because not conscious of being asleep, but sleep has many stages, and that only is perfect sleep which we call Death.

To use your expressive phrase, I am hungry for the children's little faces and have habitually to resist the power of that and other tender feelings which may not be gratified. I strive to suppress those memories which would give these bonds additional power to inflict pain, and to look only to those hopes of which man cannot deprive me, and to such relief as a record may afford in the event to which my enemies refer as a means not of learning the truth and doing justice; but of condemnation and punishment. My recent letter long and sad was designed to direct your view to the realities we have to meet, that your heart should be established by resolve equal to the worst and not be made sick by hope deferred so as to be unable to bear disappointment if it should come at last. How gladly would I shield you from every pain, your own love will tell you; that love which caused you to interpose your body to shield mine when I refused to surrender[10]. But remember that your power then was over me only, my shield is not broader now than your's was then.

Feeling the necessity for this suppression of longing affection and for the constant interposition of judgment to control it, makes me afraid to dream; and I have found two preventatives generally effectual—first, to take no tea, that is, no food in the evening—second, to sit up very late and read the dullest book in my possession. But as long as your dreams continue to be pleasant, I do not warn you off of that fairy land.

Sunday, 4 Feby. The associations of this blessed day always bring my deprivations with double force before me, but I fly to that sweet consolation that the eye which watches slumbers not, the fountain of mercy fails not, and the hand that leads and protects us reaches to every place. Under His arm I trust you and our little innocents will be kept in safety and led as His wisdom may provide to everlasting life.

I will send this letter to Macon, as from your

letter it is to be inferred that you will be there before this can reach that place. "Sister Maran" had a very pleasant well furnished house there, bequeathed to her by her Brother.[11] It may have seen sad changes since it was occupied by others[12], but her welcome and kind attentions will I am sure compensate for whatever may be wanting in other things. You will there be in the way of learning more of outside affairs than in your late residence, and will I hope have something to cheer your gloomy hours.

Mr. Schely it is to be feared will find his change other than an escape from the evils which have led to his removal. The negroes are most to be relied on where they have received least of those brought in military organizations and disbanded to find new homes. Texas I have supposed had most of that class and would in that be worse than the others. It was therefore that I hoped he would not remove his family before making a personal examination and thus comparing the evils of his old home with those of that to which he was about to fly.

Dobbin has I hope enabled you to judge satisfactorily of the situation of the children and given you at least the satisfaction of being able to see the things which when unknown were likely to receive appalling shapes. I cannot advise with you, but am comforted by my reliance on your good judgement and resolution, both exalted and sustained by intensity of interest and singleness of purpose. When our family group is in imagination gathered together with one accord to make our common supplications[13] each member stands before me with such distinctness and life as only could be understood by one of like constitutional idiosyncrasy. Except my dear "'ittie Paie" they are all unchanged, and so I wish to keep them. Under your sweet recitals of her sayings and doings little Winnie grows before me, and I try to realize her voice that I may mingle it with that which charmed me so many years ago and which through all the varied scenes of my subsequent life has been ever [*in?*] my ear, waxing sweeter, not fainter, for it does not die away in the distance. My dear Winnie it is not for me to forgive you[14], but to ask for your forgiveness. We are all weak, erring, willful, sinful creatures, I should have been less so than you being older and stronger, but in justice I feel that it was the reverse, and that it is I have to ask because I love much that much may be forgiven[15]. Of you, I have [*an*] endless succession of memories all clothed in a fond Wife's tenderness, judicious care, effective aid and graceful cheering to my heart when saddest and least attractive. Though torn from you, we are not divided, you are seen in the darkness as in the light, God has joined us and will I trust reunite us before we go hence forever. Give my tenderest love to all near and dear to me when you write to them, tell my children how much I think of them pray for them and hope from them. Kiss ittie Paie and make know [*sic*] who it is for. God bless and sustain you under your heavy burdens. Let us trust that he [*sic*] will find it expedient[16], to give to us our hearts [*sic*] desire in this world. The blackest cloud is soonest dissolved, and despair is often on the border of relief. Know that my love is always around and with you, that my prayers are fervent for you and my hopes run unceasingly to you as the rivers run to the Sea. Farewell dearest Farewell,

Devotedly your husband

Jeffn.. Davis

Letter 16
(February 17-19, 1866)

F. Monroe, Va. 17th Feby. '66

Mrs. Varina Davis

My dear Wife, your's of the 2^d & 8th Insts. were received on the 10th & 16th. My last to you was directed to Macon and this will be addressed to the same place as the time of your movements is not so definitely stated as to enable to select another place as more likely to be appropriate. I am very glad to have my big boys [*sic*] likeness and that of my dear little Lize, dear to me as if she were my own daughter and nearer to me—if that be possible than heretofore by the sad traces which care have [*sic*] left on her child like face. The sufferings of all nearest and dearest to me deaden the pain I should otherwise feel because of my own condition. Oftentimes the question occurs to me, would the spirit of vengeance be satiated by my sacrifice so that my family and countrymen would then be left in peace? If so, I trust my past life will bring others to the conclusion that is embodied [*in*] the mental answer I have so often made, and that

those who would mourn me longest, would least
expect or desire me to shrink from the purchase.
You will know how to tell my Brother of my anxieties for him, and constant regrets that I cannot be
with him to share his efforts and aid in the defence
of his just cause. Insist upon his withdrawal to some
more comfortable and healthy retreat, entrusting
the care of his affairs to some one who will follow
instructions with intelligence and partial zeal. There
would necessarily be less of information and of
interest in such an employee, but this might be more
than counterbalanced by the absence of prejudice
against him. I can imagine no reason for taking and
keeping possession of his plantation except that
of relationship to me, and this may be a continuing power in the hands of subordinate officers who
seek their own advantage. He would probably find
gratification in visiting that part of Wales from
which our ancestors migrated. A short time must
for good or evil determine the future of our section.
If there is to be disorder and carnage he and Lize
should be absent, if the present clouds blow over it
will be more pleasant to return when law and order
prevails again in the land. The men who founded
the government of the U.S. had before them the
examples of ancient republics and tried to guard
against the defects which led to their destruction
we know against what the barriers were erected and
have experience as to their efficacy in one phase, it
remains to be seen whether there are checks which
will save us from following in the downward grade,
at the foot of which lies [*sic*] the graves of former
Republics. From ancient Rome to modern Mexico
the same great blunder has caused the same sad
story to be told. May God guide those who have
in charge the heritage our Fathers left; so that they

will save it for posterity.

Mr. Minnegerode came to see me two days ago, spent several hours with me and promised to return in about three weeks. He made many friendly inquiries for you, expressed the wish he had felt to write to you and said he would if permission was given send a letter to you through the War Dept. He brought me a twig from a shrub growing over the grave of my bright and beautiful[1], also some leaves from decorations with which kind hands had dressed that little mound in which was laid so much of my tenderest love and brightest hope of earthly things. The promises which find their fulfillment in a in a [sic] better world were mingled with the memories of my buried hope. I received the sacrament[2] with comfort to my longing soul; and wait with patience for the grace to say—Not mine, but Father, thy will be done; in all thy chastening I see the evidence of love, and not knowing why, yet know that it is well, and is so ordered.

I am glad that you will see many of our relatives and that they will have a chance to see our youngest child. In after years it may be you will be more together and I trust it will be so. Please caution them as I have you against being disturbed by the stories which circulated concerning my condition. Whether idly or maliciously done it matters not as ignorantly it must be since visitors are not allowed to approach me and cannot know that of which they write. My health is now as good as usual, Dr. Cooper[3] has kindly made such changes in my food as have relieved me from the effects of indigestion and I do not realize any consequences beyond such as are attendant on close confinement. The hope which

belongs to consciousness of innocence and of
power to disprove such allegations as are supposed to have been made, or such as false witnesses may make against me sustains me still. Slanderers have now nothing to restrain or correct them
and they have not lost their opportunity to revel in
that vengeance which is indulged in with freedom
proportionate to its safety. The slip you enclosed
gave me the first information that Genl. Scott had
incorporated in his autobiography such a bald
falsehood concerning me, he however probably
did not know that so far from being the author of
"repudiation" I was never a disciple of the creed,
and he only seized on it as a good hook on which
to hang the selfish falsehood he intended to utter.
That poor little ingrate Walker[4] who had never
received any thing but benefits from me, and had
repaid them with treachery and injury (being one
of the rare occasions on which he took any heed
of his debts) is the originator of the charge against
me of repudiation; and he must have known it to
be false when he went to England to publish it,
for he was most actively engaged in Missi. politics
when the event occurred. It is true that I never
heard of Genl. Scotts [*sic*] article about Lt. Col.
John Moryellion Wilson, before I saw it referred
to in the slip; but that is not all, there could have
been no such loss as is spoken of by repudiation
of Missi. bonds. The Union Bank bonds were
those which Mi. "repudiated" and they never
were [*written over another word*] put on the market
so that individuals could have invested in them.
The Planters Bank bonds never were repudiated,
partial provision was made for them, and I always
expected they would be paid. The constitutionality of the former was more than doubtful, that

of the latter was never questioned. The doctrine
of repudiation never received any quarter from
me. I engaged in politics, after the event had transpired out of which the repudiation party arose of
"which McNutt[5] was the leader," after which the
bonds had been "repudiated", and the question
had become political merely. That the State never
accepted the doctrine of repudiation but stood
on the ground of constitutionality and only entertained the question of "debt or no debt" is my
patent in the discrimination made between between
[sic] the Planter's Bank and the Union Bank, bonds.
Many years ago on account of the unjust assaults
made on Missi. I wrote a statement of the case op-
probriously named repudiation, and published it in
the "Union" Washington D.C. It was after a vain
attempt to find what had been done with the Missi.
Union Bank bonds after the U.S. Bank of Philad
to which they belonged had gone into liquidation,
and remarks thereon excited spleen against me. I do
not recollect whether in that paper was stated the
attempt made in the mission of Robins[6] to effect
an arrangement for the payment of the Bonds by
voluntary subscription. I obtained from the State
Dept. such an introduction for him as only could be
had for one in an official or quasi official position.
This is only one of the many forms in which a low
malignity pursues me at a time when it is known I
am not allowed to vindicate myself, and it is a sad
evidence of public depravity that it can go unre-
buked by all who deserve to be called men.

Tell my dear old lion hearted Brother that such
depraved assaults can only excite my contempt,
unless they should acquire value by disturbing him,
and that I hope he will regard them merely with
the scorn which I know he would feel if they were

directed against himself.

When Mr. Harrison joins you he [*will* (*very faint*)] probably be able to give you some information and will I am sure be willing to serve you as he best may. The Clerk and Watson have a case with which you will of course not be involved.[7] The chance of doing good is so small and the soot so thick that it would be unsafe to approach. I had more confidence in the third Brother than in the other two, but my opportunity to [*judge?*] him was very limited.[8] If Jennie's Uncle has behaved correctly, he cannot allow his agent to escape upon such a pretext as that set up; if they are combined, it will delay but hardly prevent a public exposure, disgraceful to all who are connected with either. I sincerely regret having given my countenance so as to induce others to confide in them, and can only desire the fullest punishment for any breach of faith either of them may have committed. After I heard of the first defection, I was prepared for any thing but good as my remark on that occasion must have indicated.

It was a great relief to me to learn that your recent intelligence had quieted your apprehensions in regard to the children, and that will enable you to make needful arrangements before you go for an indefinite absence. My opinion is still that it will be better for you to separate yourself and the children, with a view to their proper education, it would not be pleasant and cannot be requisite to illustrate by examples. Have you thought of Hamburg as a temporary residence? Early associations are all important. Conscience, industry, perseverance, self denial are qualities which may be cultivated into fruitfulness or neglected to destruction. When I look on the likeness of my dear warm hearted boy, fervently do I pray that his walk may be such as his open brow and truthful eye promises. How much character there is in the letters formed by his little hand. I had hoped to lead him in his earlier years, upon you is devolved a double task. I do not think any thing has been lost by the training of Jeff's early years: his character indicated government through his affections and I always found them sufficient. Water cannot be solidified without freesing [*sic*], until it has been incorporated with foreign substances; it may be for crystallization, for flower or for fruit. Much knowledge must be acquired and assimilated before caution and exactness can be given to impressibility without impairing it or close analysis can be added to quick perception. To fill the heart with love for God and for man, to imbue the mind with a sense of justice, to surround it with an atmosphere of reason, to consume every prejudice by the concentrated rays of truth is the proper end of education. By instruction to direct the youthful mind towards that end, hic opus est[9].

The difference in the character of the boys will increase the difficulty of the work, but love sweetens labor. The belief remains with me that Billy was injured by the harshness of his first nurse, it will be for the tender hand of his Mother to smooth the asperity. When you visit the convent you will at once see whether our nervous, confiding little daughter has been treated as her nature requires, and it is needless to say that nothing would compensate for a different course. She comes to me when I sleep, and shadows in the day time take her form; but I will not trust myself to write as I feel about her. May the Lord guide and protect you all, and so lead us by His grace that however separated now we may be united in Him and as His own at last be gathered into the same bundle; when He shall divide the tares from the wheat[10].

18th day. Not being able to close my letter for the mail of yesterday and there being no mail today I will finish it tomorrow so as to give you the latest date. The Lental [*sic*] season does not, I understand command much attention here. I hear the [*bugle*] call for church, and on this day it always brings associations not readily dismissed from my memory.

19th day. Mrs. Clay after her return to Washington sent me a coffee pot to enable me to make coffee for myself. Dr. Cooper came and gave me full instructions as to its use making very good coffee as a part of the lecture, I have followed directions not with the best success, indeed I am led to doubt whether cooking was designed to be my vocation, but the inducement will sustain the effort and may be rewarded by giving me a new power to serve you in time to come. In your future letters please give me your address from time to time so that I may know to what place to direct the answers according to their date. When you reach Missi. you will easily learn much which will aid in deciding your course, without that information it would be worse than useless for me to express an opinion. You say you have lost the clue to the meaning of "The": add Holmes[11] and I suppose it will give it. As you requested, I sent in a previous letter a lock of hair freshly cut, if the letter is frequently viseèd [*sic*] it may be lost in which event will send you another whenever you desire it. Many thanks for the

goggles and the screens[12]. You are quite an artist
and as often before come happily to my relief. My
eyes do not suffer much from inflammation; but
the neuralgia of the head sometimes renders me
almost blind—during the paroxysm. I have chloro-
form mixed with aconite, and also a prepa[ra]tion
of SpTs [*spirits*] of Camphor which serves in the
milder attacks. If more were needed Dr. Cooper
would readily do it so far as the healing art extends, so that you may rest assured that whatever
is practicable in my present imprisonment, for the
preservation of my health is as fully done now as
when Dr. Craven was here. He has, I learn, gone
to New York to reside. The locket has not reached
me.

I recollect Frederick[13] very well, first met him
at Manassas, and had a very favorable opinion of
him. The Quadrilateral was handed to me and I
soon found what was not told—that it had been
sent by you. The author has attempted the very
difficult task of portraying the inconsistencies of
human nature, Sir Walter Scott alone has succeeded in doing it. We have as much in real life as anyone can need and in fiction we might be treated to
pictures harmonized in coloring. The disclosure of
Ida's secret and the slaughter of prisoners who had
laid down their arms could not have been done by
one as true and generous and brave as his hero is
represented. The horse is the best character in the
book as I measure them. Do you recollect "old
Duke" the horse I rode in the Pawnee campaign?
He might have stood for the portrait, except that
even in extreme age he was not gentle.

Does "Dobbin" intend to take his family back
to his old home? I have considered your remarks
about myself and as you have better opportuni-

ties to judge than myself will not reply though
not concurring in your conclusion. Sometimes
the mind becomes diseased by long dwelling on a
given subject. Sometimes shut out from observation it turns inwards with a force before unknown
and sees more in darkness than it did in light. Let
us be happy the Lord reigns, and in due time we
shall know wherefore things were done.

Kiss my baby, of whom you cannot write as
much as I wish to hear of her sayings and doings.
Say to my dear relatives and friends somewhat
of those things I have written in various letters.
I hope you will in meeting find some relief from
the isolation you have so worthily borne. May
the protector of the defenceless the refuge of the
oppressed be with you alway [*sic*; *frequently used for*
"always" in BCP].

Farewell dearest Winnie nerve your heart to
lifes [*sic*] trials as you have to its duties and let us
hopefully wait and pray—Again Farewell

Ever devotedly your Husband

Jeffn Davis

[*In his most minute handwriting, at the very bot-*
tom of the page: the usual signature above this is double
the usual size.]

P.S. If Mr. Harrison is with you give him
my sincere regard, with regret that his faith to me
should have brought him so much evil. D.[14]

Letter 17
(March 13-14, 1866)

Fortress Monroe, Va.
13th March '66

Mrs. Varina Davis

My dear Wife.. yours of the 23d with P.S. of
the 26th Ulto. and copy of Maggie's letter and four
photographs came to cheer me on Sunday last.
The photographer's [*sic*] treat you badly, even in
this copy the eyes lose much of their natural effects as shown in the miniature by being too heavily colored, but I am thankful for it as it is and for
the others also. Maggie's shows me what she is,
Ma's what she was and little Pollie's preserves the
morning of her sweet babyhood. Of the past nothing can rob me, and it rises before me now with
the vividness which only certain conditions of the
mind can give. It is often well for us that there is
a land of waking dreams, peopled with memories
robed in imagination and unrestrained by judgement.
Your reception[1] at Macon was such as I anticipated, from my own experience and it is so much

the more valuable because those friends have little demonstrativeness and no insincerity. The kind manifestations mentioned by you as made by the negro servants are not less touching than those of more cultivated persons. I liked them, and am gratified by their friendly remembrance. Whatever may be the result of the present experiment the former relation of the races was one which could only incite to harshness in a very brutal nature. I cannot believe if left to themselves that unkindness would be as frequent as where laborers and employers are of the same race. Interference by a third party especially if prejudiced or ignorant, might destroy the feeling which has heretofore subsisted and generate collisions, as well by encouraging unjust expectations, as by offering an object for opposition which by its equality with the higher race would excite its passions. Unless such change has been wrought no southern man can be excusable for arguing against the non existent intolerance on the part of the whites towards the blacks; and if such sad change has been produced it was a duty demanded by every dictate of justice, and sentiment of manhood, that he should when speaking under such circumstances, attack the cause of the evil and contend for its removal, that the normal friendly relation might be restored. In view therefore of the facts of the case as necessarily [*sic*] known to a Southern man and of the general fact, that the virtues of forbearance and charity are most useful and difficult of exercise by the dominant party, Mr. Stephens'[2] speech would have been more appropriate and of better augury if it had been made by his namesake of Pa.[3]. That great and highly commended virtue—charity—requires that we should make large allowance for

defections which are produced by timidity and
selfishness—the one disturbs reason generally,
the other tips the scale to the near side; together
they so obscure truth as to confound, for the time,
virtue and vice, faith & treachery. The manner
in which you mention the name of the organ of
Gov. B's committee[4] shows that you have Burrow's
estimate of him[5]. I knew him well, enough to feel
no surprise. If it should appear that they were
connected in those hidden cotton speculations
my opinion would be therein sustained. The last
time I saw him he was on a mission to me to get
a change of commander in Ga. & he induced my
friend Gus.[6] to urge compliance on me, and the
latter thought hardly of me for my positive refusal
to entertain the proposition. I saw speculation for
a set of men whose names were only mentioned in
connection with the public defence, I believed that
the civil and military power would be energetically
exerted to run out cotton, and for obstructing so
grand a conception can hardly hope to be forgiven
by those whose golden prospects I thus disappointed. Policy restrained me from making the explanation to Gus. and the scales may not have fallen
from his eyes even at this late day.

Has dear little Paie suffered no ill consequence of her fall? I wish I had been there.—May
the omni-present, the one who alone is good,
shield and guide you all. Don't criticize beeby's
knotty head too severely to one who has always
had difficulty from the same cause in combing the
skin of his own. I am glad she knows my likeness
it will seem to her as a memory of me and perhaps
enable her heretofore to recognize me. Your meeting with our relatives will I hope be fully related in
your hoped-for letters. The letter subsequent to the

one acknowledged by you asked for instructions as to where you should be addressed at stated times. The transit of a letter is so slow that it seems scarcely possible to reach you now en route and unless I hear from you before closing this it will be a problem as to where it should be sent. You will no doubt learn many things regarding the events of which you have written when you reach Montreal and can then judge better than now. There are however certain rules which do not vary with the merit or demerit of parties to a special case. I cannot recall "Edwina's father," and am surprised at the sudden change in the character of J's uncle, if he has behaved as reported. Poor child however unjust it may be such sins will descend and extend to all his family. The matter between him and W. had a still wider relation and coming controversies therewith connected must taint whomsoever it touches. The fall of a divided house is not more inevitable than that of a family warring within itself. Not the least of the evil effects of such a condition is the demoralizing influence it has on the younger members.

When I was not permitted to see any newspaper it was stated to me that a member of my staff had published an account of my journey after Genl. J.E. Johnston's surrender and of my capture, etc., a recent letter to the N.Y. Herald from a correspondent in Richmond Va.: reveals the fact that the soi disant[7] Aide was the clerk of the Navy Dept. of whom you heard as having gone to New York after the evacuatios of Richmond, there performing other scurvy tricks in addition to this of falsely representing himself as my Aide de Camp and companion.

But enough of the meaner things and of things rendered mean by the severe ordeal through which

all have had to pass; it is more comfortable to contemplate the gems which the bubbling cauldron
has thrown to the surface, their inherent brightness
revealed by the fierce commotion throwing off the
dregs which had incrusted them.

"As darkness shows us worlds of light

"We never saw by day. [*sic, his spacing*]
I deeply sympathize with the family of that
good friend Mr. Schley, and would that it were
in my power to do for them as he did for mine in
the hour of their distress. An inscrutable providence has snatched away from our people many
whose places could at no time have been filled,
but whose loss weighs the more heavily—for having fallen upon us "when our need was the sor-
est"[8]. The cheerful temper with which the young
men who had been reared in affluence, went to
work with their hands, gave assurance for the future; I hope the reports of growing despondence
because of political action leading to organizations for expatriation, have been exaggerated. All
cannot go and those who must stay will need the
help of all who can go away. The night may seem
long, but it is the part of fidelity to watch and
wait for the morning. It has often happened that
events which seemed to be unmixed evils have
resulted in the greatest benefit to a people, and
more often still has the success of unjust schemes
and the haughty spirit fostered by it, been the immediate precursor of a fall. Narrowing the circle
to our own family affairs you will I know be able
to draw consolation and find hope in our losses,
by reverting to former fears entertained by you in
regard to the children.

I will not repeat suggestions heretofore made in connection with subjects of apprehension; of an invasion of Canada, and the approach of cholera to this continent. Close confinement in an exterior fortress gives me very little opportunity to judge of such matters and I can only pray that your steps may be directed aright. Whatever I have said in former letters touching your movements you will of course consider by the light of all the facts known and to be learned by you. If we had the same information it is not probable that our conclusions would differ except in so far as your's may be affected by your desire to see & to serve me. Against that influence I will again warn you, it is not probable that you will receive the desired permission to visit me and you can best serve me by relieving me as far as possible from solicitude for you and our children. Our paths are widely separated but I hope they are converging towards that home where sorrow enters not, where there are no partings, where the wicked cease from troubling and the weary, weary, are at rest.[9]

14th—In the selections for the morning service of this day, I have found comforting promises and fold them to my breast close mingled with the love which neither misfortune nor suffering nor distance nor inevitable separation can darken or deprive of its warmth. Warned by a sad experience against such calculations as would make hope sanguine and expectation swift, I will yet hope though in patience and strive to find adequate protection beneath the shield of the conviction, that all things are ordered in wisdom and mercy and love, that I may fully feel "even so Father for it is thy will".[10]

The weather is warm for the season, the buds of the willows are swelling and all this suggests the fear that you will find the crowded cabin of a steam boat, in your journey to and from N.O. uncomfortable if not unhealthy. Mr. Harrison will I know do all in his power to provide for your comfort, and I feel great confidence both in his head and his heart. I once hoped to have been of service to him and much regret that the reverse has been the result of his connection with me.[11] You will probably see "Dobbin" and you know with what confidence and affection I regard him. Tell me when you learn it of the course adopted by Henny. I wish it were in my power to talk with her. Knowing her Mother very well I can perceive by what currents she is borne along, at least it so appears to me.[12]

Margaret looks ill at ease " [*sic*] dear child for very dear she was and is to me. My anxiety for her is not the less because I no longer have power to cheer or to relieve her. What has become of W.W. he has not been mentioned when you have spoken of J. at least since he was noticed as being in N.Y. The children will have so much to tell you that you will have little difficulty in learning their circumstances, but much in deciding as to the propriety of changing—In all the affairs of life we are reduced to choosing between evils, every situation having its disadvantages—you recollect the instructive satire of Horace on the desire for change—etc. The return of Jeff to the same school was I think fortunate, as it will leave you to consider of future and more permanent arrangements without the disadvantage of two removals. Nothing would to my judgement compensate in little Pollie's case for gentleness, tenderness inspiring confidence. The boys as soon as Billy is old enough should be together unless there should be some special objection—If God permits my purpose would be to have them all together and be myself with them as much as possible. Please tell them how much I think of them, pray for them and by memory bring each one into the family group to ask for us jointly that our heavenly Father if it be best for us will cause us to be reunited, and that he will give us grace so to live that we may all be forever together in Heaven. If they have the radical virtues and love one another the clouds which darken the morning of their life may be but the harbinger of a sunny day.

Remember me most affectionately to Ma. to whom I hope there are happier days in store. Tell her that the old one hit Le Roy at last, but that his faith held out and he never cried "quarter." Give my love to the girls and Fiddy when you see him. You will hear how and why he was detained and the consequences. I do not realize how it can be without appropriate remedy; but the world has been moving in courses so strange to me that I am as much lost as was Rip Van Winkle[13].

Mr. Minnigerode failed to come when he was expected and a report has reached me that he was detained by sickness. I hope it may not be serious. His kindness to me in coming so far to see me as soon as permitted, and the comfort his prayers and judicious conversations have given me, place me under a deep debt of gratitude to him.

Of myself there is nothing new to report and no data on which to base any speculations as to the future. My health is about the same as heretofore and the effect of close confinement has been less deleterious than might have been anticipated.

The account you have received of our friends who were at Fort Delaware will enable you the better to understand my situation and the change which occurred in their case[14] may perhaps come in mine. It would be taken at a venture as men do when they feel any change may improve and cannot make matters worse. Such books as are in the Post Library are freely furnished to me, they are chiefly works suited to a military man, therefore not quite such as I would choose but they serve the useful purpose of turning my thoughts from painful reflections, and are not without interest to me, though to my future life in any supposable contingency the knowledge they contain must be inapplicable. This is I believe the year in which according to calculation the worlds [sic] brotherhood is to begin, when the implements of war are to be converted into implements of agriculture[15]. Would that the rumors of war in many lands should have such blessed termination. "When things get to the worst they sometimes mend."

I am glad to hear that Genl. Lee has written an account of his campaigns[16], and hope it may be as beneficial to him as expected, but it is the benefit to the cause of truth for which I am most glad. If many officers will do likewise, the errors of various writers, viewing affairs from the various positions held by them will enable the careful historian, by comparison & correction, hereafter to give a just relation of the events of the war. When the passions of the hour shall have so far subsided as to permit wisdom to resume her judgement seat, it will be more practicable than now; and even now by easier access to the information of both sides, it is more practicable than it was during active hostilities. It is to be hoped that like attention will be given to the records of civil transactions of that time. When the veil is lifted, there will be need to cry aloud for patience and forbearance & charity and above all for charity -. And those who never wore a mask will be most prompt to practice it towards those who never were without one. Mrs. Clay is expected here daily, and I hope she may have succeeded in obtaining her Husband's release. For some time past I have not seen any notice of Mr. Mallory or Yulee and hence trust they are no longer in prison.[17] If my letter seems disjointed and obscure do not infer any physical ill as the cause. The tramping and creaking of the sentinels' boots disturb me so as to render it difficult to write at all.

[*Note: The next and last page of this letter is written crossways-on top of and at right angles to-the text of the first page. The superimposed words read as follows:*]

Farewell dear Winnie though deprived of the loving care which for more than a generation has soothed my anguish the sweet memory of it is ever with me and will cheer the few days which can at most remain of a checkered life. May angels guard you and the good Shepherd lead you along the paths that lead to peace here and happiness hereafter. When shadows fall darkest upon me then the brightness of your unfaltering devotion is most conspicuous and then most I feel how much more you gave than I deserved. May our heavenly Father reward you according to your deserts and bless our children for your sake. To divine guidance trust your steps. It never yet was sought in vain by those who sought aright.

I linger still loth to leave even this imperfect union with my most loved object yet feel that it is vain and worse than vain to struggle with a fate to which it is my duty both to bow and seek to reconcile my tenderer self. Once more dear Wife farewell my prayer continues still that you all be conducted in safety to the place where you should be and may God reunite us in this world if it so may be

Ever most affectionately and trustingly your Husband

Jeff,, Davis

Letter 18
(March 22 ,1866)

Fortress Monroe, Va.

Mrs. Varina Davis

22 March 1865
[*mistake for 1866*]

My dear Wife

I have received your's of the 8th Inst. and infer that the second letter sent to you at Macon was not received. It was addressed to the care of Genl. Cobb[1] and may reach you after being forwarded. Since that I have addressed another to you at Louisville, care of our friend Col. Johnson, supposing that your journey could not be intercepted at a more southern P.O.

The intelligence of Sister Susan's[2] continued illness gives me great anxiety and in like manner I regret the suffering of Fannie though from your statement it is inferred that the acute disease has subsided. Your remarks in regard to Joe[4] lead me to the conclusion that some former letter of your's containing an account of his troubles must have been lost on the way. I have no knowledge of the case, neither can I fix Mr. Peyton or Mr. Gartley who are mentioned in that connection. Wm. Hartley the father of Eugene I knew very well, but supposed him dead longsince [*sic*]. You will need no expression to assure you of my solicitude for Joe's welfare, but if I knew more, my power to serve him is gone.

Kiss itty Paie and tell her it is my thanks for the pretty flowers she sent me, gathered in my own country and among the singing of the birds so well remembered. The flowers preserved all their brightness and to me were eloquent, as that is measured by effect upon the feelings.

I am deeply grateful to those friends who manifested kindness to you, and realize in it that noblest sentiment of man which vindicates the oppressed. Like you I do not believe such expression would have been evoked by success, though a more noisy and more ephemeral and selfish exhibition might have waited on the possession of power. The apothegm which you cite has its secret in the different character of the followers of the banners of martyrdom and persecution. It was therefore philosophically said that the key to the different fortunes of James the second and of William the third of England, was to be found in the remark of the former that a certain person wanted to be a martyr and that he should be gratified therein and of the latter on a similar subject, that he did not intend to gratify the apparent desire to be made a martyr. And this carries me out to another train of thought. If William III [*sic*] had administered Ireland with the same forbearance and respect for right which he observed towards England, how much of suffering to one and evil agitation to both would have been avoided. How differently would the history have been written of the years which have passed since the treaty of Limerick. You will be in the midst of the excitement caused by Fenianism and which for the sake of all concerned, may I hope prove to be unfounded, and of another excitement growing only the proposition for a confederation of the provinces. A prisoner long and closely confined, I can therefore form no opinion in regard to the subjects, nor would it be proper under the circumstances for me to express one. But the shelter the Canadians have given to my unprotected family renders me too thankful to be indifferent to anything which involves their permanent prosperity and peace.

I am not surprised that you found Mrs. M. to be very handsome, if she has recovered youthful appearance. As you do not mention her Mother I suppose you did not see her, for she would surely have impressed you. To me she was one of the finest specimens of maternal dignity I have met, and according to my ideal might have sat for the Mother of the Gracchi. Nor was it only apparent as the heroic character of her sons witnesseth. The letter and handkerchief she sent me was one of the valued momentoes in my valise. Judge C. is a connection of hers, through his first wife. Is Mrs. Strickland dead? She was a very kind amiable lady, to whom I was indebted for the most friendly attentions on various occasions. But I will not rehearse the people and the places by whom and at which I have been taught how much there is of good in the world; and the memory of which has so often impressed me with the obligations imposed upon me to labor diligently to discharge somewhat of the heavy balance against me in the account with my fellow man of services received and rendered. They have generously credited me with good intentions and I believe they far exceeded my works.

Thank my true hearted friend Lamar[4] for his kind remembrance of me. I can wish him no better fortune than that his success should be equal to my estimate of him. As I acknowledge your letters by their dates you will be able to discover when one is lost, and to renew any thing to which you desired a reply and elsewhat [sic] you may be willing to rewrite. I have a sweet letter from little daughter the answers to which will be enclosed with this. There is visible improvement not only in the writing, but in the composition. The latter showing advance of thought, but not at the expense of the sincerity and purity and confidence of childhood. There are few things of which I could not write more soberly than of my little Pollie—so I desist.

I have likenesses of each of the family now except Billy. Maggie's is a copy of her miniature when an infant. Though they are not necessary to recall the appearance of any of you, I do not like when they are laid before me that Billy's shouldn't be there also. Dear little bright boy there still comes over me that feeling in regard to him heretofore described. The history you have promised to give me after seeing them will be hopefully looked for. But you must reconcile yourself to the task of writing it; and to the necessity of working without waiting for quiet. Though I am in the condition to give the highest value to quiet, it being the thing never allowed to me by day or by night, I did not suppose much abstraction to be necessary for you to write so that I could understand albeit I fear my own success is not very good in that regard. It is well for you that my writing is not in character representing sounds; and now having pointed out to you one thing in it which is well, I rest in that triumph.

Mrs. Clay arrived a few days since, she did not obtain the release of her husband on parole; but he is now allowed to go about the Fort from sunrise to sunset. She did not get leave to see <u>me</u>, and I hear will go back to Washington and further I know not. The opportunity to breathe freely the open air and to be undisturbed during the day will no doubt be serviceable to Mr. Clay's health, and it is gratifying to me that so much of relief has been accorded to one of us.

The spring is slowly appearing and as well as the calendar reminds me of the many months during which I have been closely confined without any legal proceedings or even informal notice of the charges and evidence on which I have been held as a "State prisoner". So I strive to possess my soul in patience[5] and by every means attainable to preserve my health against undermining circumstances. Your caution against <u>pork meat</u> is one easily observed, as I have so little disposition to eat meat of any kind that but for the adverse opinion of the Doctor I should at least during Lent have continued to abstain entirely. Your letter gave me the first notice of the presence of Trichimia. The theory of its origins in Germany, wanted the complement of dates and circumstances. There is a similarity which readily occurs between the condition of Germany at the close of the thirty years war, and that of the Southern states at this time. If there be no longer any doubt as to the existence of the disease and as to the cause of it, there should be inquiry and investigation into its history and characteristics, so as to avoid the carnage through which practitioners have arrived at a knowledge of several diseases in this generation. Do not permit yourself to be unhappy through fears for my health, as I have heretofore informed you [*last word written in tiny script between the lines*] the injury sustained has been less than was reasonably to have been anticipated under treatment so unusual. In the matter of diet, there is nothing now to complain of and the officers of the guard treat me with all the consideration compatible with their position. The daily walk of an hour is continued and the exercise in the open air usually revives me. So I hope long yet to be able to meet any fair ordeal, and afterwards to be serviceable to my family as opportunity permits.

I have heard nothing for a long time of the "State prisoners" confined elsewhere, and hope therefrom that they have all been released. It would not be possible for me to hear any thing which would surprise me more than the mendacity and hypocrisy of those peace stories except that in any group there should not have been some one whose recollection of events would enable him [*last word written much smaller than the others, crowded in at the end of the line*] to detect the fraud. But the whole course of that man[6] and others of his class can serve but for a very temporary delusion as a mere reference to dates will exhibit them first among the recipients of office in the organization by which they now plead they were unwillingly dragged along. Delegates to the convention which formed a provisional government, constituted themselves ex officio its congress, chose an executive and summoned him from his distant home,

and a vice Presdt. from the members of the Convention, will find it difficult to make any reasoning
being believe they were reluctantly acting under
the compulsion of those who were not present
or advising. Whosoever shall seek thus to escape
responsibility must soon meet the finger of scorn
and always feel self reproach to either or both of
which I leave the subject of the Maj.'s story. Give
my love to Ma and Maggie and Jennie if there.
Kiss the dear children for me. Tell them that I
daily bring them by memory together and with
you at the head of the group, ask petitions for us
according to our Saviour's promise. My dear Wife
though I cannot expect you to feel less anxious
for me, let me beg you to address all your energies
to the heavy task imposed on you in having sole
charge of the children. You cannot effect any thing
for me would probably meet wounding repulse
in any attempt to do so. If it be so that I can go
to you, it will involve little delay to reach you
wherever you may be, until then, seek in making
the best practicable arrangement to find the most
agreeable employment for you.

Farewell my dear Wife, may the peace of the
holy comforter be with you ever prays with all the
fervor of devoted love, your Husband

Jeffn.. Davis

Letter 19
(April 8-9, 1866)

Fortress Monroe Va.
8 April 1866

Mrs. V. Davis,

My dear Wife, your letter from N.O. of the
18th Ulto. with its enclosure came safely to hand,
to the one from Joe's I replied on the 22d Ulto.
addressing you at Montreal. The newspapers have
announced you as passing Memphis on the 31st
Ulto., and by or before this date I hope you have
joined our dear little ones in their place of refuge. I
am anxiously expecting to hear from you at points
on your journey where you had an opportunity
to write and in due time to receive intelligence of
your arrival in Canada and of the condition in
which you and our family there are [*at*] the time
of your writing. I hope little Winnie has recovered from the effects of her fever and that she may
soon be restored from the fatigues of her long
travel. The colder and drier air will I am assured
be beneficial to you and I pray that the Summer
may bring back the health and strength of which

you were deprived by the trials to which you were exposed after our separation. You need rest both for body and mind and your new situation should enable you to make such arrangements as will secure to you more of both than you have recently been able to command. You will be able to learn much which is hidden from me and to adopt such course as under the circumstances [*the "t" is not crossed*] will be advisable. I will not interfere with the exercise of your judgement by further suggestions. If the blind may not lead the blind[1], still less should they attempt [*the first two "t's" not crossed*] to lead those who have sight.

The kind remembrance of my old friends as shown to you is to me very gratifying and to them honorable. Next to the consciousness of rectitude, it is to me the greatest of earthly consolations to know that those for whom I acted and suffer approve and sympathize. It is common in cases of public calamity for those who feel the infliction to seek for some object on which to throw the blame, and rarely has it happened that the selection has been justly or generously made.

There has been no important change in my condition and the future action to be taken in my case has not been in any wise revealed to me. The recent proclamation announcing the restoration of the authority of the civil courts would seem to involve a transfer of prisoners held for trial by such courts, from military to civil custody. You will probably hear of any decision which affects me before I do, and must try to wait with such patience as is exhibited by those who have control in the matter. To you as to me there is one consolation, it is hardly possible that any change should not be for the better. You evince a purpose to seek for permission to visit me here, but I think you had better wait for further developments. You will recollect former remarks in this connection, and will readily perceive how much more was thought than it was supposed I would be permitted to write. Instead of reasoning from general data, you should refer to your own experience and so much as you know of mine, during the past year.

If the letter which you no doubt wrote to me from Vicksburg should not reach me, I hope you will repeat your account of our relations in that section, and such news as you got in regard to our negroes. Poor things if they heard of your arrival I have no doubt all who could do so, came to see you and the baby. Judge Sharkey[2], could tell the Congressmen of things which would be more beneficial to the negroes in our neighborhood, than agents and civil endowments.

The V.B.s must all be what my Brother thought W. was some years ago.[3] I am pleased that you made no reply and the more so because it indicates the course you will pursue in all similar cases. Though we may not judge[4] we may avoid the goats, when they have been set apart by proofs of a satisfactory nature to show the proper dividing line.

The reports of Fennian expeditions[5] continue as news items in the papers and I wish there were less possibility of disturbance in the quarter to which you have gone. It may well be that my ignorance of passing events causes my apprehension, obscurity being quite as essential to the terrible as to the sublime. The agitated condition of many civilized [places?] makes it difficult to say where one would find a land of peaceful quiet, if free to choose and possessed of the wings of a dove[6]. May the Lord guide you and shield you and our little ones from all danger and adversities.

Dr. Cooper brought his little daughter to see me, a sweet child who Mr. Clay had told him looked like Maggie, there is some resemblance and still more to Ellen's Jennie it seems to me. The Dr. recollects you in Washington[7]. Dr. Craven was here yesterday, he did not see me and I am sure it was not from indifference on his part. It would have been very gratifying to me to have seen him and to have heard of his kind Wife and Daughter. I can never be less grateful for their attentions than when like the good Samaritan they gave me relief and proved that I had not passed the limit of humanity. Benefits are to be measured by the motive with which they are conferred and by the effect which they produce. I therefore feel deeply indebted to the Dr. and the Ladies of his family, for a benevolence which had much to suppress and nothing selfish to excite it, and but for which my captivity would soon have ended in death. If their own good hearts have caused them to reject the base slanders and false accusations made against me, I trust they will yet have conclusive confirmation of that belief.

We have had a few warm days here, it is now as it was yesterday, cool and raining. The swallows sing in token of coming summer, but the trees like Govr. Marcy[8], do "not respond at all." Your trip has been through so many degrees of latitude that I had hoped the spring would have opened before your journey was closed. The sententious Roman claimed that man might at least be allowed the wisdom of a migratory bird, and therein, I think, committed the error of claiming for reason, more of certainty than belongs to instinct. Greater extension it has, but within its narrow and special channel instinct seems to me more unerring. The rod of the water-seeker may dip where there is no vein, except that of wonderful credulity, but the roots of a willow will run towards the water.

9th I have thought in the right season of the joy which your meeting with the children would give to all and prayed that the Lord would give you strength to dismiss for the time repining on account of my absence, and grace to accept the dispensation with the christian humility which murmurs at nothing which He ordains. It is not given to us to know wherefore but faith enables us to say it is well, the judge of all the earth cannot do wrong. I see them clinging to you with trusting love, & you looking down on them with maternal pride, let not my shadow cast gloom on the bright picture. Though I would that I were with you, looking beyond myself I rejoice in your gladness and feel that I cannot be sad if those far dearer to me than myself are happy.

    The letter from my little Pollie is a sweet graceful image of her honest, affectionate heart I am sure she will be a comfort and honor to her family in after years. My generous, headlong "Big-boy" may not meet your wishes in his progress at school, but habits of study may be gradually acquired if not too eagerly pressed at first, and time is often gained by waiting.[9] My dear little Billy will soon be old enough to go to school with his Brother and the association will I hope be mutually advantageous to them[10]. That unaccountable anxiety for him haunts me still. And does not little Winnie exult in her large train of loving hearts? There is one more than she numbers to be added.

Give my love to Ma and to Maggie and to
Jennie[11], if with them.

It will no doubt be a great gratification to
Ma. to hear of her friends in New Orleans and to
know the things which you can tell her of there-
abouts. Such repast in a modified form I anticipate
when your letter from Vicksburg shall reach me.
Remember but two have come since you left Ga..
One from Joe's and one from N O. As you said
nothing in the last, of Jackson it has occurred to
me that you had probably written from there. I am
thus particular that you may know whether there
is any thing you would be willing to repeat.

Mr. Minnigerode was accidentally prevented
from visiting me week before last, but has announced his purpose to come during this week.
He is kindly anxious and his conversations are
to always [*sic*] desirable. No other person from
the outer world has been allowed to visit me as a
friend. Tell Jefferson that I often repeat that hymn
remembering that he does so likewise, and hope
it may all be realized to him, and to us all both in
time and Eternity.

Evening. My dear Wife, though I long to see your
loved face and to hear your loving voice again,
I must dissuade you from your purpose to apply
in person, for permission to visit me under existing circumstances. You would probably be disappointed and your grief thereby rendered more
poignant, but worse than even that, you would be
exposed to the prying curiosity and the heartless
vulgarity of the scavengers of the press, who cater
to the unmanly malice which has so long and un-
scrupulously assailed me; but if hope and love will
see over these barriers, and if the permission were

given, new trials, to which I may say nothing for my own gratification would induce me to subject you, would await us here. It is not probable that the present state of affairs will long continue, and you will more to do [*sic*] than can soon be accomplished. May our Heavenly Father give us patience under our affliction & sanctify it to our good.

If I have time before closing this to write a note to my dear daughter in reply to her, you will please hand it to her, if not tell her I was most gratified to receive a letter from her in French, a later one had been already answered, with my last to you directed to Montreal.

Farewell dear Wife, sadly do I write again farewell and prayerfully trust that the day is not remote when a more cheerful word may be spoken to you, and our separation be at end. Kiss our children for me; my love is ever with you, devotedly clinging to the happy memories of our younger days & assuring me of one thing, which though earthly is unchanging.—Farewell, yr. Husband

JeffnDavis

Letter 20
(April 21-23, 1866)

F. Monroe, 21st April 1866

Mrs. Varina Davis

My dear Wife, your welcome and anxiously looked for letter of the 12th Inst. reached me on the 18th by which time according to the newspapers you had reached Montreal. In the joy of your reunion with the children I rejoice, finding in the event your common happiness and welfare. Of myself I have little to say; in that as in some other aspects bearing resemblance to that knife-grinder.[1] The happiest event for me which has occurred here was the release of my friend and fellow sufferer Mr. Clay. He was not allowed to take leave of me and his Wife I suppose was unable to obtain the permission she sought to visit me. Dr. Minnigerode visited me a few days since, full of the Christian and humane love which my sufferings have led him to make more manifest than in the time of my prosperity. Do not be distressed about my health, there is no cause for alarm, as there is no active disease and the change is so

slow that I expect to be on hand like MaCawber
[*sic*].[2]

It is a great comfort to me to know that kind
hearts greeted you and smoothed your path in
your late journey. I hope the burthens imposed
on you because you were my Wife will not be
renewed, and that the memory of noble sympathy
which then thought to relieve, will be crowned
by such manly generosity towards you hereafter,
that you will realize humanity to be the rule and
brutality the exception. The photographs were
more grateful to me than you seemed to expect. I
had none of Billy and his look always rose before
me with appealing expression. Maggie does not
look well, she is too thin and what is the meaning
of the swollen lip? It would be useless to suggest
to you close inquiry and observation as to her
food and exercise. Perhaps her ambition has been
so stimulated as to cause her to study too many
hours, and thus to rob youth of its requirements,
and spread over childhood the sereness [*sic*] that
only withering years should bring. On this and all
else, you will have to see, to reflect, and to judge
for yourself.

Thank you for the cheer you gave my dear old
Brother, and hope he will join you this summer
at some place suitable for both of you. I will not
repeat cautions as to cholera, though my anxiety
increases in relation to it. Do you recollect Dr.
Cartwright's treatment? Do not disregard my addition to his prescription— Carbonate of ammo-
nia—nor rely on opium.

Dear little Lize, who could be otherwise
than gentle to her. You do not mention Florida
or Joe M. nor Julia's child named for me.[3] This is
not complaint, because you promised fuller ac-

count when you had better opportunity to write, but a reminder. Did Mr. Porterfield leave his family independent. His means were large but I fear his books were loosely kept and his agents badly chosen. The box containing your likeness did not come, on the letter was endorsed "no box recd. J.S.."[4] Mr. Harrison has acted as I expected, he has my thanks mingled with regrets that my hopes of serving him in his future career should have been not only disappointed but that the association should have been to him a misfortune.

The young Soldiers who saw you in the [*train*] cars at Binghampton reported the interview and described how bright and wide awake little Winnie was. It was a great pleasure to me to hear an eye witness. The weather is quite warm, the earth is clothed in her bright robes of promise, the birds sing joyously, and I will not like the Bard of Avon complain that they are tuneful while "I so weary fu' o' care".[5] Though not the voice I long to hear I draw from it the pleasure it was designed to give by the beauteous creator who did not mean that man's happiness should be at the mercy of man; and therefore formed him for companionship with nature and endowed his soul with capacity to feed our hopes which live beyond this fleeting life.

By the newspapers you will have seen that a committee of Congress is engaged in an inquiry into the charges against me, on which it appears I have been so many months kept in close confinement. This is probably the new reading of the Constitution and the exemplification of civil rights. Good may come out of evil, and in this case if truthful witnesses are called or perjured informers revealed, good must result. Still reliant

on the shield of innocence, I say to you be hopeful and wait in patience.

Have you read the "Diary of Kitty Trevyl-
lian"? The Capt. in many traits reminded me
of one dear to you and not less honored by me.
The book did not seem to me equal to the "Cotta
Family," but the subject was not of such thrilling
interest. As I cannot send this tomorrow (Sunday)
I will postpone the conclusion so as to give you a
later date, to me there is nothing new, but another
day, another link added to the lengthening chain
of our separation.

Sunday—Glorious day which gave the last proof
of the Redeemer's divinity and the first guarantee
of Man's justification and mediatorial protection.
Blessed hope that we are to be judged by Him who
bore every human affliction for our salvation, and
having felt all the emotions of human affection,
can sympathize with those who suffer, and pardon
the errors of our better [*bitter?*] nature. Who that
reflects on man's judgment can fail to look out
from its corruption and weakness, with desire to
meet the judge who cannot err? Often has it occurred in the world's history that fidelity has been
treated as a crime and true faith punished as trea-
son. So it cannot be before the Judge to whom all
hearts are open, from whom no secrets are hid.[6]

Dr. Cooper has just been to visit me, he says
all which is needful for me is air and exercise. It
was the want which Cowper's kind bird had, and
hardly has bird more usually sought for air and
motion than I did, when I had Byron's "heritage
of woe".[7] But I am not of Cato's creed, and do not
hold that it is man's wisdom to equal the swallow,
but man's dignity [*this word is written very large, over*

an erasure] to bear up against trials, under which the lower animals would sink. Resolution of will may not, according to Father Timon, prolong indefinitely our earthly existence, but will do much to sustain the tottering machine beyond the observer's calculation. I look forward to the day when I shall see my Winnie again, and again with our beloved little ones live the life of which the world knew not, and which was more than all beside, to me.

I will enclose with this a letter and check sent to me for you, with acknowledgement appended. You will take such further action as to you may seem best. The motive claimed grateful acknowledgement, the amount did not indicate the propriety of refusal, but the rather suggested, such act might be misconstrued.

Give my love to Ma, Maggie and the children. To your letter from Montreal, I will look for information concerning them. The Baby will no doubt be quite a heroine with the other children and be surprised at the interest they take in her. God bless and guide you all, until in His good pleasure and by such paths as He may choose, you shall assemble in the mansions of bliss, prepared before the foundations of the earth were laid. How small, how poor are the contentions and objects of this world, when compared with the eternity to which we are hastening. There oh! Father let us be gathered together, loving there as we loved here, save the earthly imperfections & fears.

23rd—Yesterday an officer who knew Mr. Brodhead[8] mentioned a report that something was the matter with his Son, my surprise probably suppressed a fuller statement. Please tell me if there be truth in this one of many ramifications of slanderous malignity. You can imagine how one shut out from all direct communication with his friends dwells upon every shadow and longs for light.

Tell me as much as you can of the sayings... doings and looks of the children. Let not the anxiety for the absent cloud the joy which your reunion is capable of bringing to you & to them. It is no misfortune to you that care and responsibility for others will occupy you, and in useful effort may the Lord give you comfort. Yesterday my walk was extended to two hours, and I hope for continuance of the extension as the good Doctor has urged the necessity for more air and exercise—Fear not but trust in our almighty Protector and receive his dispensations as the decrees both of wisdom and love. Give my most affectionate remembrance to all our family and receive the warmest aspirations of the heart which is devotedly your's as it has been these many years—Your Husband

Jefferson Davis

Untranscribed note from JD to Varina.

Endnotes

Letter 1

1. Judge James Speed, Attorney General since Dec. 1864.
2. Brierfield.
3. Joseph Emory Davis (1784-1870), the sole surviving brother, out of four.
4. Three out of five are still living: Anna, Lucinda, and Amanda; He may write only to his wife, Varina.
5. *Papers of Jefferson Davis (Papers of JD)* 12:18 n. 11 identifies as Jefferson Davis Van Benthuysen, nephew of Eliza (Mrs. J. E.) Davis.
6. Ellen and Jim were servants.
7. Macon, Georgia.
8. Raleigh, North Carolina.
9. Book of Common Prayer (*BCP*).
10. Psalm 27:16, *BCP.*
11. This prayer ends both Morning and Evening Prayer, *BCP*.
12. Winnie (a.k.a. VHD, big Winnie)-his nickname for Varina, his wife; Polly (a.k.a. Maggie, Pollie)-Margaret, his daughter; Big-boy (Jeff)-son Jefferson Jr.; Billie (a.k.a. Button, Billy)-son William Howell; L.P. (a.k.a. Li'l Pie, Piecake, P.C., little Winnie, little V., 'ittie Pie Davy, Paie)-family names for baby Varina Anne; Aunty (a.k.a. Marga)-Varina's sister, Margaret Howell; "the Little man"-son Samuel Emory, their first child, who died in his second year.
13. "O thou great Jehovah."
14. "Whene'er the angry passions rise", *BCP.*
15. Regimental.
16. Savannah (often abbreviated as Savnh) Georgia (Ga).
17. Richmond, Virginia; the Confederate capital.
18. An adage quoted by Laurence Sterne, a favorite author of Davis's, in *A Sentimental Journey* (1768).
19. John 14:2; Phil. 4:7; also in *BCP.*

Letter 2

1. Latin: short for ultimo (in the month before).
2. Commander at Fortress Monroe.
3. French: up-to-date.
3. A key word in the "Prayer of St. Chrystostom" (*BCP*).
5. Latin: in the place of a parent.
6. Become known (Webster: transpire, v.i., 2).
7. Genls. J.E. Johnston and W.T. Sherman; they had agreed to an armistice.
8. Bumble, in Dickens's *Oliver Twist*, sets his own worth at "six tea-spoons, a pair of sugar-tongs, and a milk-pot; with (some) second-hand furniture, and twenty pound in money" (See Chaps. 23 and 32).
9. *Papers of JD* 12:28 says it was Jefferson Davis Howell, VHD's little brother.
10. Joseph Robert Davis was JD's nephew. JD is referring to the surrender of Gen. R. E. Lee at Appomatox Court House.
11. Burdens.

Letter 3

1. Latin: short for instant (in the same month).
2. Augusta, Georgia.
3. A servant.
4. See p. 173 ref. to hymn about "angry passions" in Letter 1, p. 4 (Aug. 21, 1865).
5. Slave houses.
6. Hurricane; Brierfield; Diamond Place (*Papers of JD* 12:38).
7. The Davises' housekeeper.
8. Baltimore (Balto); Richmond (Richd).
9. "my little friend" refers to Dr. Cravens's daughter, Anna.
10. Mary Jane Bradford Brodhead, daughter of JD's sister, Amanda.
11. John Mitchell, an Irish leader and journalist.

Letter 4

1. Luke 21:19.

2. At West Point, after an accident.

3. Holly Springs, Mississippi (JD's abreviation-Missi.).

4. Hurricane mansion was Brother Joe's plantation adjoining JD's at Davis Bend on Mississippi River which was burned and its contents destroyed.

5. He never was after 1815.

6. Joe. Smith, son of JD's sister, Anna.

7. Watson Van Benthuysen, nephew to J.E. Davis's wife.

8. William Howell, VHD's brother.

9. Probably the *New York Herald* since it is cited in *Papers of JD* 12:38 n. 18.

10. sacrifiée; G., an artist friend, says a figure put into a picture to enhance the main one, instead loses out completely (See VHD to JD Sept. 22, 1865 in *Papers of JD* 12:28).

11. From a "song" by Robert Burns, a favorite poet of JD's.

12. Mildred Lee was the youngest child of Gen. R.E. and Mary C. Lee. Custis is her brother and had served JD as aide-de-camp during the War.

13. *The Suffering Savior: Meditations on the Last Days of Christ* by the Revd. Dr. F.W. Krummacher.

14. Reference to Jesus Christ.

15. In Great Britain.

16. Sir Henry Vane and the Duke of Argyle were both anti-royalists; both were executed.

17. In saying, "Father, forgive them"?

18. From Sophocles, *Antigone*.

19. Mr. & Mrs. Burt Armistead.

20. George Schley housed VHD, Piecake, a nurse, and Margaret Howell for months.

21. Sister Lucinda was m. to Wm. Stamps, lived at the home place, Rosemont.

22. Joseph Smith.

23. Encountered in his U.S. Army days in the West.

24. Latin: Rather, mens sana in corpore sana ("a sound mind in a sound body"; Juvenal, *Satires*, #10).

Letter 5

1. "that the Lord would give father something which he could eat . . . and bring him back to us with his good senses to his little children, for Christ's sake", then Maggie would "quit the table to dry her tears": from VHD, *Jefferson Davis A Memoir*, II, 714.
2. Joe. Davis & Smith.
3. All these services, prayers, and readings are in *BCP*.
4. See Felicity Allen, *Jefferson Davis, Unconquerable Heart*, App: C..
5. French: As for the rest.
6. Thomas Jordan, "Jefferson Davis" (*Harper's New Monthly Magazine*, Oct. 1865, 610-20).

Letter 6

1. Joseph.
2. Georgia and Alabama.
3. George Bancroft's *History of the United States.*
4. Regiment.
5. Adopted sons of J.E. Davis's d. Florida and husband.
6. James Seddon, Sec. of War CSA.
7. Latin: in the state in which (we left her).
8. Anne's.
9. Burt Armistead.
10. Mrs. Howell Cobb.
11. John Taylor Wood.
12. An abortive raid across the U.S. border into Canada near Buffalo on June 1, 1866 was the only activity of these Irish nationalists near this time.
13. John Wood and Preston Johnston.

Letter 7

1. Luke 21:19.
2. *BCP.*
3. Job 3:17.
4. Mary Ahearn, Pie's nursemaid.
5. Matt: 6:25-34.

6. *The Faithful Promiser*, by the Rev. J.D. McDuff, was a popular devotional book.
7. Ben Hill; Bson may be Burrow, their nickname for Cobb.
8. Brig. Gen. James Chesnut.

Letter 8

1. Shenstone was an 18th century English landscape gardener and poet.
2. Psalm 120:4, *BCP.*
3. Robert Burns, "Tam O'Shanter."

Letter 9

1. She was almost 60 years old.
2. Mathew 13:24-30.
3. Commanding Officer.
4. Chesapeake Bay.
5. Alfred, Lord Tennyson, "In Memoriam."
6. *The Gayworthys* was a current novel by A.D.T. Whitney.
7. "History must be false."
8. Joseph E. Davis.
9. French: it doesn't matter.
10. Philadelphia.
11. Thomas J. Wharton; Secretary of State William H. Seward.

Letter 10

1. Archbishop Connoly of Halifax has offered to educate both Jeff Jr. and Maggie (Pollie).
2. Luke 10:30-37.
3. John Reagan, Postmaster-General, CSA; Massachusetts, in 1865; see *Papers of JD* 12:74 n. 5.
4. Stephen R. Mallory, Secretaries of Navy, CSA.
5. George Davis, Attorney General, CSA; North Carolina.
6. Cf. I Kings 19:10, 14.
7. Virginia Clay.
8. David Hume.

9. Dr. Edward M. Goulburn, a conservative Anglican priest. See *Papers of JD* 12:75 nn. 13, 15.

10. Matt. 18:23-35.

11. See, e.g., I Cor. 10:13.

12. Headquarters.

13. James Lyons and his wife were close friends of the Davises' (*Papers of JD* 12:75-76, nn. 21, 22).

14. G.W. Huntington; purchase was 'a thousand cigars' (*ibid*, n. 23).

15. Latin: Experience keeps a dear school, but fools will learn in no other.

16. See P*apers of JD* 12:76 n. 26.

17. James Guthrie, an old friend of JD (*Papers of JD* 5:71).

18. Mr. Buchanan's *Administration on the Eve of the Rebellion.*

19. Matt 26:39-44.

20. Psalm 35:11.

21. Montgomery, Alabama was the first capital of CSA.

22. John Wood, Preston Johnston.

23. "not stolen . . . Robert took them."-VHD to JD, Dec. 1865 (*Papers of JD* 12:80).

24. Burton Harrison (his private secretary) and Frank R. Lubbock (his Aide-de-camp); both were captured with JD and were imprisoned separately.

25. VHD expects to visit the Cobbs in Athens, Georgia (*Ibid.* 78 n. 40).

26. Genl. Beauregard.

27. Col. L.B. Northrop, Commissary General of CSA and a personal friend of JD.

Letter 11

1. The Kentucky grammar school he attended taught by Dominicans.

2. JD visited Havanna in 1835.

3. French: my first love.

4. This is the reading. It is not "Ma."

5. Cf. Psalm 50:10; John 10:1-16, I Peter 2:25, 5:2-4.

6. I John 3:23.
7. See Phil. 3:7-8; writing "o" instead of "a" in "gain" imitates
   .Irish brogue.
8. From "Te Deum laudamus" in *BCP*.
9. Jefferson Davis Howell (a.k.a. Jeddy, Fiddy), Varina's youngest
   brother, JD's namesake; naval cadet, CSA, at war's end.
10. Warship commissioned by the CSA; sunk by U.S. Navy off
    Cherbourg, France, June 19, 1864; another brother, Becket
    Howell, was an officer on it.
11. Minnie Leacock Howell, the elder brother's wife; his Mother
    was Margaret Louisa Kempe (Mrs. W.B.) Howell, the "Ma"
    of these letters.
12. 1858-59.
13. Frank Lubbock and Burton Harrison.
14. Colonel William Preston Johnston and his parents, Gen.
    Albert Sidney and Henrietta Johnston; ASJ was JD's best
    friend at West Point.
15. In Charles Dickens's *The Pickwick Papers*.
16. For "affectionately."

Letter 12

1. Feast day, *BCP* Dec. 26.
2. With whose parents Varina was living in Georgia.
3. Latin: (written in small letters, partly between the lines) The
   conquering side was pleasing to the gods, the conquered one,
   to Cato (who killed himself because of the defeat).
4. Schley proposes moving there.
5. Freedmen's bureau?
6. Hurricane? & Brierfield?
7. Beulah Howell Glasser, born 1783 (*Papers of JD* 12:97).
8. Jefferson Davis Howell.
9. Watson Van Benthuysen, nephew to J.E. Davis's wife: British
   pronunciation of the word "clerk" gives us the very cogno-
   men of Watson's opponent (Micajah Clark) and an example
   of JD's subtle and quiet humor; Clark was his chief clerk
   while president: see *Papers of JD* 12:81, 228, 245-47, 267.

10. I.e., for daily prayers with him, as he describes in Letter 1 and mentions in Letter 2.

11. "the terrible thirst for your blood" See *Papers of JD* 12:81.

12. Anna Davis Smith, his oldest sister, still living.

Letter 13

1. Last two words supplied from *Papers of JD* 12:98.

2. For identity of these people, see *Papers of JD* 12:102-03, nn. 4-6.

3. Dr. Samuel A. Cartwright, 1793-1863: a Mississippi friend of JD; see *ibid.*, n. 8.

4. Land.

5. This time, definitely this form.

6. J.R. Macduff, a Scottish minister whose books of fiction and poetry as well as religion were selling by the millions in the U.S.A. and Great Britain. *Papers of JD* 12:104 n. 14.

7. "for the Promotion of Evangelical Knowledge" (*Ibid.*).

8. R.M.T. Hunter.

9. Mr. Alexander Stephens, V.P. of the CSA.

10. Lord Richard Howe; Great Britain.

11. This probably refers to the disastrous invasion of Tennessee in the fall of 1864, planned by Gens. Beauregard and Hood; but often blamed on JD. Hardee and Cobb were old friends of JD, and so probably knew the truth of the matter.

12. The Smith land.

13. South Carolina.

14. A hypocrite in Dickens's novel, *David Copperfield* (1859).

Letter 14

1. Possible reference to her sister Margaret.

2. Eccles. 1:9.

3. Lize Mitchell, Joseph Davis's granddaughter.

4. Freedmen's Bureau.

5. Lt. Gen. Wade Hampton.

6. In an 1814 tale by Chamisso.

7. By Colfax.

8. Member of the House, soon to be Speaker.

9. Original: "leisure" (Psalm 27:16, *BCP*).
10. Psalm 143:8.
11. Matthew 18:19.
12. H. was one of the disbanded Conf. soldiers driving a wagon for VHD when they were all captured in Georgia.
13. His sister Anna Smith's home in Louisiana.
14. Cf. Heb. 13:6; from Thomas à Kempis, Imitation of Christ.
15. Psalm 88:8.
16. Discharge from prison of East Tennessee Unionist W.G. Brownlow.

Letter 15

1. The Rector of St. Paul's Episcopal Church, Richmond, Virginia, where the Davises were communicants.
2. Cf. Prov. 3:17.
3. Cass Lewis (1782-1866), served as a general in War of 1812; governor of Michigan as Territory, then as State; Senator; Sec. of War; U.S. minister to France (1836-1842); Democratic nominee for president 1848 (defeated by Z. Taylor); Sec. of State 1857; author of books on American Indians and on the French govt.
4. John L. Crittenden; Crittenden Compromise committee.
5. James Buchanan (1791-1868), politician and diplomat; served long terms in both House and Senate; as Sec. of State under Polk, settled the Oregon border dispute with England; elected Pres. of U.S. in 1856.
6. Franklin, in whose cabinet JD served; Before JD's release in May of 1867, Peirce visited him in the prison several times.
7. Mr. Leonard is the husband of J.E. Davis's daughter, Caroline; Norfolk, Virginia.
8. The key word in "A Prayer of St. Chrysostom," *BCP*.
9. Popular devotional books by a Scottish minister, J.R. MacDuff.
10. In the Georgia woods.
11. Mary Ann Lamar (Mrs. Howell) Cobb.; her brother, John Lamar, who died in the War.
12. I.e., Union officers: see *Papers of JD* 12:118 n. 36

13. Preceding 8 words from "Prayer of St. Chrysostom", *BCP*.
14. As she asks in her letter of Jan. 22-24 (Davis Coll., U.
    of Ala.).
15. Cf. Luke 2:36-50.
16. St. Chrysostom's word again (*BCP*).

Letter 16

1. Son Joseph Evan Davis, b. 1859; killed 1864 in a fall at the
    Conf. White House in Richmond.
2. Holy Communion.
3. Dr. George E Cooper, replaced Dr. Craven in Dec., 1865.
4. Robert J. Walker.
5. Alexander G. McNutt.
6. Thomas E. Robins, nephew in-law to JD.
7. M.H. Clark and Watson Van Benthuysen.
8. Jefferson Davis Van B. (1840-1872); see *Papers of JD* 12:18 n.
    11; Mrs. Joseph E. Davis was their aunt.
9. Virgil, *Aeneid*: this is our task.
10. Matt. 13:24-30, 36- 43.
11. Theophilus Hunter Holmes was a friend from army days.
12. Masks for his eyes.
13. Frederick Maginnis, a mulatto who has offered his service
    gratis to VHD.
14. Burton Harrison had been entrusted with getting Varina and
    the children out of Richmond. This done, he rejoined JD
    and was captured with him, jailed in Washington, then Fort
    Delaware, and only recently freed.

Letter 17

1. By the Howell Cobbs.
2. Alexander H. Stephens.
3. Pennsylvania; i.e., Thaddeus Stevens (1792-1868), Senator
    and Radical.
4. Gov. Brown's committee was investigating JD's finances.
5. O. A. Lochrane; see nn. in *Papers of JD* 12:132.
6. Augustus H. Kenan (*Papers of JD* 12:132 n. 14).

7.French: self-styled.

8.Sir Walter Scott, "The Lady of the Lake," Canto 3, Stanza
  16, ll. 3-4

9. Job 3:17; it is JD who doubles the word "weary."

10. Matt. 26:39; Mark 14:36.

11. The U.S. imprisoned Harrison for many months as a suspect
    in the Lincoln murder.

12. Henny was sister to W. P. Johnston, daughter of Henrietta and
    Albert Sydney Johnston, JD's most intimate friends in his
    youth.

13. Character who slept for twenty years in the Washington Irving
    story of that name.

14. B.N. Harrison & F.R. Lubbock; I.e., their release.

15.Cf., e.g, Isa. 2:3-4.

16. General R.E. Lee; a false rumor/he had only begun it when
    he died.

17. S.R. Mallory (Sec. of Navy, CSA); David Yulee.

Letter 18

1. General Howell Cobb.

2. Widow of his brother, Isaac.

3. J.R. Davis?

4. L.Q.C..

5. Luke 21:19.

6. A.H. Stephens?

Letter 19

1. Luke 6:39.

2. Wm. L., a noted Miss. justice.

3. Van Benthuysens, brother and nephews of Eliza (Mrs. Joseph)
   Davis; Watson?

4. Matt. 7:1.

5. See above Letters 6 and 18.

6. Cf. Psalm 55:5-7

7. I.e., before the war.

8. Gov. Wm. L. of N.Y., 1833-1838.

9. Jeff was never a good student and died at age 21.

10. William died at the age of 11 from a childhood disease.

11. Sisters of VHD.

Letter 20

1. A satiric character in "The Friend of Man and the Knife-
   Grinder," published 1797 in *The Anti-Jacobin* (*Papers of JD*
   12:76 n. 26).

2. Mr. MiCawber is in Dickens' novel, *David Copperfield.*

3. Joe Davis's daughter and husband; J.D. Porterfield.

4. James Speed.

5. Bard of Avon is a reference to Shakespeare. JD mistakenly
   applies the name to Robert Burns; quote from Robert Burns,
   "The Banks o' Doon."

6. From the opening Collect in the Holy Communion service,
   BCP.

7. "On a Goldfinch Starved to Death in a Cage" by William
   Cowper (pron., "Cooper"); George Gordon, Lord Byron,
   "Lara."

1.2, Davis, a superb horseman, was known for his afternoon rides
   around Richmond, for relaxation.

8. Richard Broadhead, a nephew-in-law, or his father.